Helsinki Travel Guide, Finland

Touristic Information

Author
David Mills.

SONITTEC PUBLISHING. All rights reserved. No part of this publication may be reproduced, distributed, or transmitted in any form or by any means, including photocopying, recording, or other electronic or mechanical methods, without the prior written permission of the publisher, except in the case of brief quotations embodied in critical reviews and certain other noncommercial uses permitted by copyright law. For permission requests, write to the publisher, addressed "Attention: Permissions Coordinator," at the address below.

Copyright © 2019 Sonittec Publishing
All Rights Reserved

First Printed: 2019.

Publisher:
SONITTEC LTD
College House, 2nd
Floor
17 King Edwards
Road,
Ruislip
London
HA4 7AE

Table of Content

SUMMARY	1
INTRODUCTION	4
HISTORY	8
TRAVEL AND TOURISM	16
QUICT GUIDE	18
Getting in	18
Getting around	31
Seeing	59
Buying	100
Eating	111
Drinking	134
Stay safe	163
Respect	167
Contact	168
SIGHTSEEING IN HELSINKI	170
FAMILY TRIP WITH KIDS	182
CUISINE & RESTAURANTS	186
TRADITIONS & LIFESTYLE	191
CULTURE: SIGHTS TO VISIT	197
ATTRACTIONS & NIGHTLIFE	202
Other Attrations	207
Veuve Cliquot VIP Experience SkyWheel Helsinki	207
10 GREAT SUMMER ACTIVITIES FOR HELSINKI	211
TIPS FOR TOURISTS	220
UNUSUAL WEEKEND	223
CLIMATE	226
ACCOMMODATION	228
Extraordinary hotels	228
Stylish Design Hotels	232
Luxury and fashionable hotels	236
Hotels with History	240
Legends Hotels	244
Romantic Hotels	248
SHOPPING IN HELSINKI	252

Summary

The world is a book and those who do not travel read only one page.

It is indeed very unfortunate that some people feel traveling is a sheer waste of time, energy and money. Some also find traveling an extremely boring activity. Nevertheless, a good majority of people across the world prefer traveling, rather than staying inside the confined spaces of their homes. They love to explore new places, meet new people, and see things that they would not find in their homelands. It is this very popular attitude that has made tourism, one of the most profitable, commercial sectors in the world.

People travel for various reasons. Some travel for work, others for fun, and some for finding mental peace. Though every person may have his/her own reason to go on a journey, it is essential to note that traveling, in itself, has some inherent advantages. For one, for some days getting away from everyday routine is a pleasant change. It not only refreshes one's body, but also mind and soul. Traveling to a distant place and doing exciting things that are not thought of otherwise, can rejuvenate a person, who then returns home, ready to take on new and more difficult challenges in life and work. It makes a person forget his worries, problems, frustrations, and fears, albeit for some time. It gives him a chance to think wisely and constructively. Traveling also helps to heal; it can mend a broken heart.

For many people, traveling is a way to attain knowledge, and perhaps, a quest to find answers to their questions. For this, many people prefer to go to faraway and isolated places. For believers, it is a search for God and to gain higher knowledge; for others, it is a search for inner peace. They might or might not find what they are looking for, but such an experience certainly enriches their lives

Introduction

A city of the sea, Helsinki was built along a series of oddly shaped peninsulas and islands jutting into the Baltic coast along the Gulf of Finland. Streets and avenues curve around bays, bridges reach to nearby islands, and ferries ply among offshore islands.

Having grown dramatically since World War II, Helsinki now absorbs more than one-tenth of the Finnish population. The metro area covers 764 square km (474 square miles) and 315 islands. Most sights, hotels, and restaurants cluster on one peninsula, forming a compact central hub. The greater Helsinki metropolitan area, which includes Espoo and Vantaa, has a total population of more than a million people.

Helsinki is a relatively young city compared with other European capitals. In the 16th century, King Gustav Vasa of Sweden decided to woo trade from the Estonian city of Tallinn and thus challenge the Hanseatic League's monopoly on Baltic trade. Accordingly, he commanded the people of four Finnish towns to pack up their belongings and relocate to the rapids on the River Vantaa. The new town, founded on June 12, 1550, was named Helsinki.

For three centuries, Helsinki (Helsingfors in Swedish) had its ups and downs as a trading town. Turku, to the west, remained Finland's capital and intellectual center. However, Helsinki's fortunes improved when Finland fell under Russian rule as an autonomous grand duchy. Czar Alexander I wanted Finland's political center closer to Russia and, in 1812, selected Helsinki as the new capital. Shortly afterward, Turku suffered a disastrous fire, forcing the university to move to Helsinki. The town's future was secure.

Just before the czar's proclamation, a fire destroyed many of Helsinki's traditional wooden structures, precipitating the construction of new buildings suitable for a nation's capital. The German-born architect Carl Ludvig Engel was commissioned to rebuild the city, and as a result, Helsinki has some of the purest neoclassical architecture in the world. Add to this foundation the influence of Stockholm and St. Petersburg with the local inspiration of 20th-century Finnish design, and the result is a European capital city that is as architecturally eye-catching as it is distinct from other Scandinavian capitals. You are bound to discover endless engaging details—a grimacing gargoyle; a foursome of males supporting a balcony's weight on their shoulders; a building painted in striking colors with contrasting flowers in the windows. The city's 400 or so parks make it particularly inviting in summer.

Today, Helsinki is still a meeting point of eastern and western Europe, which is reflected in its cosmopolitan image, the influx of Russians and Estonians, and generally multilingual population. Outdoor summer bars ("terrassit" as the locals call them) and cafés in the city center are perfect for people watching on a summer afternoon.

History

The town of Helsinki was founded by King Gustavus Vasa of Sweden (which Finland belonged to for many centuries) as a new trading post in southern Finland and a competitor to Tallinn in Estonia, the Hanseatic city on the opposite shore of the Gulf of Finland. The King then ordered the burghers of Rauma, Ulvila, Porvoo and Tammisaari to move to Helsinki; the date on which this order was issued, 12.6.1550, is regarded as the date on which the city was founded.

Growth was slow, for despite the King's order, the medieval trading traditions were slow to change. Due to the wars in Russia, the Baltic countries and Germany, Helsinki was nevertheless a strategic military centre, a point of embarkation for troops and a winter haven for the navy.

In time, the site of the town on the mouth of the River Vantaa proved unfavourable, and in 1640 a decision was made to move it further south to the Vironniemi headland, nowadays known as Kruununhaka near the city centre.

Russia's growing power in the 18th century and the founding of its new capital, St. Petersburg, not far from the Finnish border in 1703 were to have a decisive influence on the growth and future of the Finnish capital. The century was, however, one of great hardship for Finland and Helsinki, which suffered gravely from war, plague and hunger. The Russians occupied Helsinki during the Great Hate of 1713-21 and again in 1742. Sweden lost its status as a superpower.

The war having been lost, it became vital for Sweden to fortify Helsinki. In 1748, construction of the magnificent sea-fortress of Suomenlinna, built on an outlying island, was begun, creating what was described by a historian of the time as the "Gibraltar of the North." The building of Suomenlinna marked a turning point in the history of Helsinki, bringing prosperity to the town. Seafaring also grew to new proportions.

In 1808 Sweden was forced to declare war on Russia as a result of the power politics of Napoleon and tsar Alexander I. Helsinki was occupied in the early days of the war and the Suomenlinna fortress surrendered. Finland was annexed to Russia as an Autonomous Grand Duchy in 1809.

Helsinki becomes the Capital of Finland

For the town founded by Gustavus Vasa, the war was a major turning point. Helsinki was proclaimed the Finnish capital in 1812 and Finland's only university, which had been founded in Turku in 1640, was transferred to Helsinki in 1828.

Devastated by fire, the town was completely rebuilt in a style worthy of a capital. Placed in charge of the rebuilding project were Johan Albrecht Ehrenström, a native of Helsinki, and the German-born architect Carl Ludwig Engel, who together gave the city its monumental Empire-style centre. The most conspicuous building in the Empire centre is the Cathedral, completed in 1852.

Helsinki soon became an administrative, university and garrison town, and the biggest industrial city in the land. By the beginning of the 20th century it had a population of over 100,000.

The links with the provinces and foreign countries vital for an industrial city were forged with the building of railways to Hämeenlinna in 1862 and to St. Petersburg in 1870. The late 19th century architecture reflects the rise of industrialism, of growing affluence and European trends, the most imposing examples being the neorenaissance buildings along Esplanadi, Aleksanterinkatu, Mannerheimintie and Erottaja. The

Orthodox Uspensky Cathedral, the largest orthodox church in Western Europe, was inaugurated in 1868.

The first Finnish opera was performed in 1852 and opera took on national importance. The music of celebrated Finnish composer Jean Sibelius figured prominently at the turn of the century, in Finland's drive for autonomy against growing Russian encroachment. The architecture of the turn of the century is in national romantic style. From this period date the Jugend, or art nouveau, districts of Katajanokka, Eira and Ullanlinna.

The independent republic

Finland declared its independence in 1917. This was immediately followed by civil war. At the end of January 1918, the government was forced to flee Helsinki. In May 1918 the war ended with victory for the government troops, led by General C.G.E. Mannerheim (1867-1951). The end of the war posed many challenges for the capital of the young, independent republic.

The independent republic developed briskly during the 1920s. The architecture of the 1920s and 1930s was marked by classicism and functionalism and was manifest in the new districts of Töölö. Helsinki Olympic Stadium was completed in 1938, but the games were postponed due to the war; Helsinki went on to host the games in 1952.

The Soviet Union attacked Finland on November 30, 1939. During the Winter War of 1939-40 and the Continuation War of 1941-44 Helsinki was attacked from the air but luckily suffered relatively little damage. Unlike all other states on the European continent that were involved in the Second World War, Finland was never occupied by foreign forces. Finland is one of the very few European countries with an unbroken record of democratic rule from the end of the First World War to the present.

In the post-war years agrarian Finland was rapidly transformed in only a few decades into a modern industrial land. People left the rural regions in large numbers to settle abroad, in the towns of Southern Finland and the Helsinki Region. Under pressure to provide housing for the steadily expanding population, Helsinki quickly founded suburbs, such as Herttoniemi and Maunula in the 1950s, Pihlajamäki in the 1960s.

The best-known modern Finnish architect is Alvar Aalto, whose works in Helsinki include the Social Insurance Institution building, the Academic Bookstore, the House of Culture and Finlandia Hall (completed in 1971).

The new Opera house by the architects Hyvämäki, Karhunen and Parkkinen was opened in 1993, and the Museum of Contemporary Art, designed by architect Stephen Holl, was opened in 1998.

Helsinki has ample experience of hosting major political conferences. In 1975, Helsinki hosted the Conference on Security and Cooperation in Europe (CSCE). The first U.S.-Soviet summit took place in Helsinki in 1990, when President George Bush met President Mikhail Gorbachev.

Finland became a member of the European Union in 1995, once again marking the start of a new era for the capital. Helsinki was one of the nine European Cities of Culture for the year 2000. In that year Helsinki celebrated its 450th anniversary, too.

David Mills

Travel and Tourism

A modern city featuring some of the most distinctive architecture in the world, both old and new, Helsinki is one of the cultural hot spots of Northern Europe. An idealholiday destination for both for lovers of the arts and those who relish its exciting and vibrant nightlife, Helsinki is also a child-friendly city perfect for family vacations, and being surrounded by forests, lakes and the sea, it is also a haven for outdoor enthusiasts.

Situated on the Baltic Sea, Finland's capital, Helsinki, is a modern city of over half a million people, and is the second most northern capital in Europe. Surrounded by an archipelago of hundreds of tiny islands, and culturally influenced by both the East and West, Helsinki is unique, combining both modern and historic architectural styles with a love of open spaces that is at the very heart of Finnish identity. See our recommendations and tourism guide to Helsinki!

Helsinki is world famous for its architecture; the city centre is renowned for its neoclassicalism, especially around Senate Square. Close by on a hilltop stands the Uspenski Cathedral, Europe's largest Russian Orthodox church, and a stunning example of the Byzantine-Russian style. Scattered about the city are fine examples of Jugendstil, or Art Nouveau. Elsewhere, the Temppeliaukio Church and Finlandia Hall represent early Modernism.

As befits one of Europe's foremost capital cities, Helsinki is vibrant, yet as laid-back as the Finns who call it home. Wide and spacious streets and avenues allow for a multitude of cafes and restaurants to serve outdoors, where you sit back and relax, and at night there is no shortage of bars, clubs and venues to choose from. Throughout the year, Helsinki offers an incredible variety of activities for people of all ages, whether they prefer challenging sports, or gentle investigations of the natural beauty all around them. Cruises around the archipelago, trekking in the nearby forests, and traditional Finnish saunas, are some of the more popular choices, but there's plenty more besides.

Quict Guide

Getting in

By plane

All international and domestic flights land at the compact, modern and airy Helsinki-Vantaa International Airport (IATA: HEL, ICAO: EFHK), which is located in Vantaa, 18 kilometers to the north of the central Helsinki. Note that in recent years the airport has become crowded, so expect delays when going through security, particularly during the Scandinavian summer holiday period. There are two adjacent terminals, connected by a short walkway:

- ➤ T1: SAS, Blue1 and other Star Alliance airlines (except Turkish Airlines in T2).

> T2: Finnair, OneWorld partners, KLM, Norwegian and most other airlines.

Taxi from the airport

Regular taxis to the center cost €30–50 and elsewhere about €8–€12 plus €1.40–€1.60/km. There is 4 taxi lines at the airport terminals: lines for the companies Lähitaksi, Taksi Helsinki and Vantaan taksi, and one line for all other companies. The price differences for Lähitaksi, Taksi Helsinki and Vantaan taksi are small: the fixed price to Helsinki city center varies for example between €39 and €43. There is an electronic sign at each of the three lines listing the current prices.

For the taxis in the fourth line there is no price ceiling, so it is extremely important that you check carefully the price before boarding the taxi. None of the taxis will probably be a scam, but it's still good to verify beforehand that the taxi isn't a scam. By law the taxi driver has to tell you if the trip will cost more than €100, but otherwise there aren't any regulations.

- Shared Airport Taxi (tel. 0600 555 555 for bookings) mini-vans start from €29 for two (mind that infants count as an adult.)

- Yellow Line is a good, cost-effective option for getting from the airport to the city center. Minivans carry up to seven or eight passengers and drop passengers off at their individual destinations. The shuttles can be found at their bright yellow desks in arrivals lounges 1 and 2. Prices start from €29 for one or two passengers and varies based on the number of people in the van.

Public transport from the airport
A new ring rail connection to Helsinki opened in July 2015. The trains run in a loop, with I-trains going east and P-trains going west from the airport. The trip takes approximately 30 minutes. The trains run every ten minutes during peak hours, but during the night service is much more limited.

The intermodal Journey Planner is your essential tool for getting around Helsinki with public transport.

Tickets from the airport
Passengers need a regional ticket costing 5.50 euros.

You can buy the ticket from a kiosk or a ticket machine. You can buy the ticket from the blue HSL machines. You can not buy the ticket from the green VR machines. The VR machines are for travelling with the trains to destinations outside the metropolitan area.

At the aiport you can buy this from a blue machine outside the airport exit/station entrance (with a cr card) or from the R-kioski kiosks (also with cash). If you are buying the ticket from R-kioski, you can buy a ticket also for your return. If you are buying it from a machine, it will be valid immediately and you can't therefore buy a ticket for your return.

For your return, if haven't already bought a return ticket, you can buy it from a blue machine on the platform at the central train station (with a cr card), from an R-kioski, the kiosk at the central railway station, a tourist information point or from the Stockmann department store.

If you have a HSL travel card, you can buy the ticket on the train itself using the machines.

Tickets bought from any ticket machines are valid immediately. Tickets bought from kiosks, tourist information points and Stockmann are bought beforehand and punched/activated on the train.

Day tickets can be bought for 1-7 days, either only for transport inside Helsinki, or the area of Helsinki, Espoo, Kauniainen, Vantaa, the airport being located in Vantaa. Check the current pricing in order to know whether it's cheper to buy a day ticket including the airport or whether it's cheaper to buy a day ticket for Helsinki + tickets from and to the airport. All touristy places are in Helsinki.

- A day ticket for 24 hours can be bought at the airport in the R-kioski and in the blue ticket machines.
- A day ticket for 2 to 7 days can be bought at the airport in the R-kioski.
- Day tickets can also be bought at for example tourist information points and the Stockmann department store.
- 24 h tickets bought from any ticket machines are valid immediately. All other tickets are bought beforehand and punched/activated on the train, tram or bus, or before entering the metro station or Suomenlinna ferry.
- Therefore, if the ticket isn't a 24 h tickets bought from a ticket machine, and you haven't activated it, you will be levied an inspection fee of €80.

Bus routes from the airport

Regional buses are no longer recommended, although there is 615 or 415 (€5.50, every 30 min), 40 min to the

Helsinki Central Railway Station in the heart of Helsinki. The bus route goes through a residential area and takes time. The price includes onward transfers by tram, bus, metro, local train, etc. Both buses leave from platform 2 at terminal T1 and platform 21 at terminal T2. Tickets can be bought from the driver. To get to Helsinki city center from the airport you need to buy a regional ticket, because the airport is actually not located in Helsinki, but the neighboring city of Vantaa.

Finnair City Bus (€6.30, every 15 min, includes free wifi), about 35 min to Central Railway Station via Scandic Continental Hotel. Cr cards accepted, slightly faster and uses luxury coaches, but no further connections included in the ticket price.

Bus lines 561 and 562 to other destinations than the city center. 561 will terminate at Itäkeskus and 562 at Mellunmäki.

Sleep between flights
If you need a place to sleep between flights, there are several reasonable hotels in or very near the airport:

Hotel GLO Helsinki Airport, Helsinki-Vantaa Airport Terminal 2, +358 103 444 600 (, fax: + 358 103 444 601), . The only hotel located in the airport building itself, on the service floor of Terminal 2 and with direct indoor access from Terminal 1.Day Rooms are also made available for use, depending on the booking situation, between 9:00 - 19:00.

Best Western Airport Hotel Pilotti, Veromäentie 1, +358 9 3294800 (, fax: +358 9 329 481 00), . Best Western Airport Hotel Pilotti is located in Vantaa, within 5-minute drive from Helsinki-Vantaa airport and within walking distance to Jumbo shopping centre and new Flamingo Spa. There is a regular bus service between Helsinki-Vantaa airport and the hotel.

Airport Hotel Bonus Inn, Elannontie 9 (Pakkala exit from Ring III Highway), +358-9-825511 (, fax: +358-9-82551818), . Friendly family-owned hotel with basic but very clean and comfortable rooms. Restaurant, sauna (evening only), free shuttle service to airport (5-7 min). €120.

Cumulus Airport Hotel, Robert Huberin tie 4, +358-9-41577100, . Mid-range Finnish chain hotel, 10 min away by free shuttle bus. Renovated in 2007. €120.

Hilton Helsinki-Vantaa Airport, +358-9-73220, . Full-service hotel right next to the airport, opened in late 2007. Soundproof windows, bar, restaurant, sauna. €150.

For general aviation (small planes) the Helsinki-Malmi Airport (: HEM, : EFHF) is available, with fuel and customs facilities available at the airport.

Finally, from some points in Europe, it may be cheaper overall to fly with Ryanair/Wizz Air to Tampere, Turku or Lappeenranta (2 hours away by train) or even to Tallinn, Estonia or Stockholm, Sweden a short ferry ride away.

By train
All long-distance trains throughout Finland and the Russian cities of Moscow and Saint Petersburg terminate in the heart of the city at the Rautatieasema (Central Railway Station). This station also provides

easy interchange to the metro and tram lines. All the trains except Allegro also stop at Pasila station, which is the last station before Central Railway Station. From Pasila you can change to tram and bus lines.

By car

Expressways connect Helsinki to Turku to the west, Tampere and Lahti to the north, and to Porvoo and towards Saint Petersburg in the east.

By bus

Long-distance national and international buses terminate at the new underground Central Bus Station (*Linja-autoasema*) in the Kamppi Center (*Kampin Keskus*). The station is adjacent to Mannerheimintie, directly connected to the Kamppi metro station and within a short walking distance from the Central Railway Station.

Low-cost bus operator Onnibus operates many lines and are rapidly expanding their connection network. Check latest information on connections from their site . Prices start from as low as 3 EUR (if booked in advance). All Onnibus buses nowadays depart from Kamppi but make sure to check the site for any changes.

For travel from St. Petersburg (Russia), Russian minibuses depart from the Oktyabrskaya Hotel (opp Moskovsky train station) three times a day (typically 7AM, 9PM and 11PM) and arrive behind Tennispalatsi at Eteläinen Rautatiekatu 8, one block away from Kamppi, early in the morning. Departures back start around 11AM in the morning (typically 11AM, 3PM and 8PM). Other minibuses are parked along Fredrikinkatu, with the departure time and price often posted on them. The trip costs around 10 euros, making this by far the cheapest option, but the buses are cramped and uncomfortable and some of them stop at numerous supermarkets on the way so that Russian passengers can go for tax-free shopping. Do not expect drivers to speak anything but Russian. The border crossing time might be substantially longer than with regular buses.

By boat

Helsinki is well connected with ferry services to Tallinn (Estonia) and Stockholm (Sweden), and there are limited services to Travemünde & Rostock, Germany as well as Gdynia, Poland. Scheduled service to St. Petersburg (Russia) operates again since April 2010, and there are occasional winter/summer cruises.

Ferries arrive at three harbours with five terminals:

West Harbour (*Länsisatama*) - Tyynenmerenkatu 8 - Tallink ships M/S Star, M/S Baltic Queen, M/S Superstar, Eckerö Line ship M/S Finlandia to Tallinn. St. Peter Line ships Pricess Maria and Princess Anastasia use the West Terminal also. The terminal has luggage lockers, café, a trolley rental, kiosk, a restaurant, public transport ticket machine, bank, an ATM and the Eckerö Line and Tallink Silja Oy service points. Tram line 7 and 6T goes from the harbour to Central Railway Station and Kallio.

South Harbour (*Eteläsatama*) - Olympia Terminal - Olympiaranta 1 - West shore of the bay. Tallink Silja cruise ferries M/S Silja Serenade and M/S Silja Symphony dock at Olympia Terminal. The terminal has a money exchange, an ATM, luggage lockers, a trolley rental, a restaurant, kiosk, and the Silja Line service point. Served by trams 2 and 3.

<u>South Harbour</u> (*Eteläsatama*) - Makasiini Terminal - Eteläranta 7 - West shore of the bay. Linda Line fast catamarans M/S Merilin and M/S Karolin arrive to Makasiini Terminal during open water season. The terminal has a kiosk, currency exchange, luggage lockers and Linda Line and Silja Line service points. Served by trams 2 and 3, or just walk to Market Square.

<u>South Harbour</u> (*Eteläsatama*) - Katajanokka Terminal - Katajanokanlaituri 8 - Right shore of the bay. Viking Line ships (M/S Gabriella, M/S Mariella, M/S Viking XPRS) arrive at Katajanokka Terminal. The terminal has a restaurant, kiosk, an ATM, a currency exchange, luggage lockers, and the Viking Line service point. The terminus of tram 5 is in front of the terminal. Trams

only depart from the terminal at 10-12AM, 3-5 and 8-9PM.

<u>Vuosaari Harbour</u> (*Vuosaaren satama*) - Hansa Terminal - Provianttikatu 5 - Mainly a cargo port, but used also by Finnlines services to Rostock, Gdynia and Travemünde and Tallink Silja to Rostock. Take metro to Vuosaari and continue by bus 90 or 90A towards "Vuosaaren satama"

See the Port of Helsinki for the latest details.

Getting around

Central Helsinki is rather compact and can be explored by foot by energetic visitors. A combination of walking and public transportation might be most convenient to cover the sights in Helsinki. HSL provides the successful Journey planner , an intermodal journey planner for public transport of greater metropolitan area of Helsinki free of charge and free of ads ever since 2001. Also cycling route finding is provided by the Journey Planner.

HSL is leading the work on an implementation of the routefinder with copyleft code and open data (interchange) standards. The latest demo can be seen at matka.hsl.fi and it has location awareness and map service as of 2015.

By public transportation

Tickets
All public transportation within Helsinki, Espoo, Vantaa and Kauniainen is coordinated by HSL .

You can opt for the Helsinki Card (1 day €46, children €23, to 3 days €66, children €33) , which in addition to public transport in the municipality of Helsinki also offers free admission to a number of museums and attractions, including all museums, a sightseeing bus and a canal route by boat. The public transport ticket is not valid to the airport, since the airport is located outside of the municipality.

The following basic ticket types are available:

Tram ticket (*raitiovaunulippu*) (€2,50 from ticket machines, travel card button with a tram symbol €1,70, *not* available from the driver) valid for one hour on trams only

Single ticket (*kertalippu*) (€2,90 by mobile phone, ticket machines or from kiosks and service points, €3,20 from the driver, travel card button "1" €2,20) valid on all HSL services within city limits for one hour.

Regional ticket (*seutulippu*) (€5,50, travel card button "2" €4,20) valid for 80 mins within and between Helsinki, Espoo, Vantaa and Kauniainen

Full region ticket (€8,00, travel card button "3" €6,30) the above plus Kerava, Sipoo, Kirkkonummi, Tuusula and Siuntio.

Day ticket (*matkailijalippu*) (€9,00 in ticket machines, R-kiosks, HSL offices and from the driver) valid on all HSL services within city limits for 24 hours. Each additional day costs €5,00. if you are travelling outside of Helsinki, to the airport or Espoo for example, you can buy a regional 24-hour ticket for 14 €.

The Single ticket allows you to travel by any local public transportation method (buses, trains, trams, metro, Suomenlinna ferry) within the boundaries of Helsinki. The Regional ticket covers any public transportation method within the boundaries of Helsinki, Vantaa, Espoo and Kauniainen. However, if you purchase a Tram ticket, you are allowed to travel only by tram. All tickets allow unlimited transfers within their validity periods and regions. Children under 7 travel free, while tickets for children under 16 are half price.

Fares can be paid by cash when boarding a bus. Otherwise the following applies:

You can buy the ticket from a kiosk, a ticket machine or a parking ticket machine. At places such as the airport you can buy the ticket from the blue HSL machines, but not the green VR machines. The VR machines are for travelling with the trains to destinations outside the metropolitan area. All commuter train and metro stations have at least one vending machine. Only some tram stops have a machine, such as the stops next to railway station or Senaatintori (the historical main square of Helsinki). Otherwise tickets for the tram must be bought from kiosks or parking ticket machines. Parking ticket machines are marked on maps on the tram stops. There is parking ticket machines at for example Pohjoiseplanadi and Eteläesplanadi, and you can buy tram tickets from these.

If you have a HSL travel card, you can buy the ticket on the train or tram itself using the machines, or in the small machine at the start of the metro station escalator or at the entrance of the Suomenlinna ferry.

Tickets bought from any ticket machines are valid immediately. Tickets bought from kiosks, tourist information points and Stockmann are bought beforehand and punched/activated on the means of transport or before entering the platform, depending on the mode of transport.

Day tickets can be bought for 1-7 days, either only for transport inside Helsinki, or the area of Helsinki, Espoo,

Kauniainen, Vantaa, the airport being located in Vantaa. Check the current pricing in order to know whether it's cheper to buy a day ticket including the airport or whether it's cheaper to buy a day ticket for Helsinki + tickets from and to the airport. All touristy places are in Helsinki.

A day ticket for 24 hours can be bought in R-kioski, , Stockmann, tourist information points, the HSL ticket machines, parking ticket machines and from a bus driver.

A day ticket for 2 to 7 days can be bought at R-kioski, , Stockmann and tourist information points.

Your hotel or cruise ship may also sometimes sell day tickets in the reception.

24 h tickets bought from any ticket machines are valid immediately. All other tickets are bought beforehand and punched/activated on the train, tram or bus, or before entering the metro station or Suomenlinna ferry.

Therefore, if the ticket isn't a 24 h tickets bought from a ticket machine, and you haven't activated it, you will be levied an inspection fee of €80.

A modern option for travel card and paper tickets is the mobile app . The prices of single tickets are the same as when using a travel card, the only downside being that the tram ticket is not available, and the prices for day tickets are the same as for all other day tickets. The mobile app could be convenient if you for example do not know where the nearest parking ticket machine or kiosk is when using a tram. You must enter your cr card information, buy the ticket and wait for confirmation before you board the train, tram or ferry, or enter the metro station area. Otherwise you will be fined €80, if you are still in the process of buying the ticket, or bought it after you boarded the vehicle/entered the area and the inspector notices this.

You can buy a single ticket for Helsinki by sending a text message A1 to 16355 (valid on trams, metro, the

Suomenlinna ferry and some buses), but this requires requires a Finnish SIM card.

You can buy a Travel Card (*matkakortti*), a reloadable smartcard sold at the R-kiosks and HSL offices, very similar to London's Oyster card. The Travel Card costs €5 (nonrefundable) and gives a 25% discount on single tickets. You can not buy tickets for 1 to 7 days with the card, only single tickets.

When using the card, you must first choose the desired ticket type, then confirm by pressing ok and finally show the card. Hold the card without pressing anything to see the remaining value or to register a transfer. One unadvertised but handy feature of the card is that it can be used by multiple people at once —. First choose the desired ticket, then press the small + symbol with a person on it, choose how many tickets you need, confirm with ok, and show the card. In case you have already bought one ticket, you are not able to buy more tickets during the validity of the first ticket, so be careful to buy the desired amount of tickets at once.

The shortest possible period with the travel card is 14 days. For example 14 days for the municipality of Helsinki costs €69.30. Season tickets are more expensive for non-residents as the prices for residents are subsidized from tax revenues; for example 14 days in Helsinki for a resident in HSL area costs only €28.70. All fares can be seen at , remember to look at the fares for non-residents.

About the transportation itself
The very useful HSL Journey Planner will get you from a street address, place or sight to another by suggesting possible public transport connections, covering the entire metropolitan Helsinki region. Try eg. "Airport" or "Railway station" for place names. It is also available in several third party mobile apps for most smart phones, which can use GPS to find your current location.

Getting around at night can be a bit tricky, as most trains and trams stop before midnight and the buses before 2AM. A limited night bus network, all leaving from the city center, runs until 2AM, on weekends and nights before public holidays also after 2AM. Services are replaced mainly by buses departing to suburbs from Kampin paikallisliikenneterminaali, Elielinaukio, Rautatientori and Postitalo.

Kampin paikallisliikenneterminaali (literally local traffic terminal) is about half a kilometre west from the central railway station inside a shopping mall. The address for the night entrance is Narinkka 1. Do not take the escalator down from the entrance - it leads to the terminal for long-distance buses and your bus will likely depart from the terminal for local traffic. Watch out for the signs saying paikallisliikenneterminaali. There is, however, long-distance buses that accept HSL travel cards, so if the travel planner Reittiopas.fi is saying that you should use a long-distance bus, use one.

- ➤ Elielinaukio is a large terminal on the west side of the railroad station.

- ➤ Rautatientori is a large terminal on the east side of the railroad station.

- ➤ Postitalo is a yellow large building on the west side of the railroad station. The stop is on the southern side of the building, between the department store of Sokos and Postitalo.

There is also two lines running within inner Helsinki and serving areas not served by suburban buses, the lines 18N and 23N. 18N departs from "Kamppi (M)", from the Kamppi shopping mall but not from the terminal within the shopping mall, instead departing from a stop on the west side of the shopping mall on the street Fredrikinkatu. 23N departs from Rautatientori, but not from the terminal, instead departing from the street Kaivokatu in northbound direction and street Mikonkatu in westbound direction. 23N serves for example the bar district of Kallio.

Check the night connections to your area beforehand if you are residing outside the city center.

There are no ticket checks when getting on the metro, trains, trams or the Suomenlinna ferry, but ticket inspectors in blue uniforms do random checks on board. If you choose to ride without a ticket, watch out for the inspectors, as getting caught without a ticket results in an €80 fine plus the ticket price.

Trams
For tourists the most convenient and scenic means of travel is the extensive tramnetwork, especially lines 2 and 3 that together do a figure-eight circuit around the city. (Both run the length of the loop, the tram just changes signs halfway through.) Trams and HKL offices usually stock an informative leaflet listing attractions along the way. There is also a free Helsinki Sightseeing 2 Tram Audio Guide available for downloading here:

The tram network is currently undergoing expansion and restructuring. You should consider obtaining an updated tram map from Helsinki tourist info or from HSL, the local public transport authority.

Buses
While the trams operate in the city center, buses cover the rest of the city. The main stations for northbound and eastbound buses are on the two squares adjacent to the Central Railway Station: Eliel Square (*Elielinaukio*) and Railway Square (*Rautatientori*). Some buses operate from the underground bus station in the Kamppi Center which is adjacent to the Kamppi metro station.

Buses are always entered through the front door and exited through the middle and back doors. When getting on the bus with a ticket you have bought earlier, you need to show it to the driver. If you don't have a ticket, you can buy one from the driver in cash (but don't try to use a bill larger than €20, the drivers may sometimes refuse large bills). If you are using a travel card, follow the instructions given above.

Metro

A metro line runs from the Matinkylä suburb in Espoo in the west, through the city center, and then to the eastern suburbs. Apart from the metro stops at the shopping centers of Iso Omena (Matinkylä), Ainoa (Tapiola) and Itis (Itäkeskus), the Rastila camping site and Aurinkolahti Beach, few places along the line are of interest to tourists. After Itäkeskus in the east, the line splits in two, with one line going to Mellunmäki and the other to Vuosaari. From the city center, the travel time to the ends of each of the lines is about 20 minutes.

Local train
VR's suburban trains operate north from the Central Railway Station, branching out in three directions. HSL tickets are valid on local trains in Espoo, Helsinki, Järvenpää, Kauniainen, Kerava, Sipoo, Siuntio, Tuusula and Vantaa. The local trains are mainly of intestest to tourists when travelling to and from the airport.

Suomenlinna ferry
The HSL ferry to Suomenlinna from the Market Square (Kauppatori) is a cheap and popular summer getaway.

Another HSL operated ferry, mostly used only by the island's residents, leaves from the eastern end of Katajanokka, an ordinary residential area from the 1980s. This ferry is a good option at warm beautiful summer days, as it will never have queues to it. In weekends, however, you have to use the Kauppatori ferry, since the Katajanokka ferry operates only weekdays. The Katajanokka ferry can incorporate several trucks, while the Kauppatori ferry is mainly intended for passengers, incorporating 1 or 2 passenger cars. The Kauppatori ferry has better views, so it's recommended to use it for one trip if you use the Katajanokka ferry for the other trip. The Kauppatori ferry departs from Suomenlinnan päälaituri (literally main pier) and the Katajanokka ferry from Suomenlinnan huoltolaituri (literally maintenance pier) at the islands, the piers having different locations.

In addition, private operators provide ferries to Suomenlinna and various other islands during the summer; however, schedules can be sparse. These departure from Kauppatori and the largest private operators are JT-Line (https://www.jt-line.fi/eng/) and Suomen Saaristokuljetus (http://www.suomensaaristokuljetus.fi/frontpage/).

The operator JT-Line operates to Suomenlinna. In Suomenlinna the private ferries dock also on the southern end of the islands, while the public ferries have their two terminals only at the northern end of the islands (which is closer to Kauppatori and Katajanokka). If you do not have the energy to walk back to the northern end once you have reached the southern end, you could take the private ferry from there and buy a ticket for the trip onboard. The southern end pier is named King's Port / Kuninkaanportti in the timetables.

Helsinki card, HSL's single ticket, day ticket, mobile phone app ticket and SMS ticket are all valid also on the HSL Suomenlinna ferry, but not on the private ferry.

There is also ferries to a number of other islands that have less to see than Suomenlinna, but may provide for example a possibility to grill on an open fire or camp overnight, both of which are forbidden in Suomenlinna. These include islands such as Isosaari, Pihlajasaari, Vallisaari and several islands on the eastern archipelago route of Suomen Saaristokuljetus. Check beforehand what each island has to offer: Vartiosaari has for example 50 villas from the beginning of the 20th century and forest, Pihlajasaari has a beach and grilling and camping possiblity but no buildings except 2 or 3, and Vartiosaari has none of the amenities Pihlajasaari has.

By taxi
Regular taxis cost about €8–€12 plus €1.40–€1.60/km. The price differences for companies such as FixuTaxi, Lähitaksi, Taksi Helsinki and Vantaan taksi are small: the fixed price from the airport to Helsinki city center varies for example between €35 and €43. However, there is no price ceiling for taxis at all, so it is extremely

important that you check carefully the price before boarding the taxi. Your taxi will probably not be a scam, even though if it wouldn't be one of these companies that owns the taxi, but it's still good to verify beforehand that the taxi isn't a scam. By law the taxi driver have to tell you if the trip will cost more than €100, but otherwise there aren't any regulations.

Here is some phone numbers and prices. Notice that the charge for waiting and slow driving is traditionally listed as simply charge for waiting in the respective sites, but it's always also a slow driving fee.

There is also mobile phone apps in addition to the phone numbers. In the app you can typically

- locate yourself on a map and choose that as your starting point
- see where the car that accepted your order is currently
- see a price estimate or choose a fixed price.

- FixuTaxi, Lähitaksi and Taksi Helsinki can be ordered by using their own apps.

- In the municipality of Helsinki you can order a Taksi Helsinki taxi with the app Valopilkku, and the app Valopilkku can be used in most municipalities outside the metropolitan area. In the other metropolitan area municipalities than Helsinki, Valopilkku can't be used. This is due to the combination that Lähitaksi had an monopoly status in these munipalities and it does not take part in the app.

FixuTaxi, +358 100 6060

FixuTaxi uses cheap Toyota cars, while Lähitaksi and Taksi Helsinki use typically new Mercedes-Benz or Volvo cars. The starting fee at for example on a weekday afternoon is €0.55 cheaper than the starting price for Lähitaksi, so the choice is mainly whether you will pay €0.55 for a luxurious car or not.

> Mon through Fri 6 am to 8 pm, Saturdays and eves of holidays 6 am to 4 pm €2.95

> Other times €4.50

> Charge for waiting and slow driving 47.04 €/h

Travel fare:

> 1 to 6 people 1.60 €/km

> More than 6 people 2.23 €/km

Lähitaksi, +358 100 7300
This is the former monopoly in the metropolitan area for other municipalities than Helsinki. The cars can nowadays also start from the municipality of Helsinki, but the availability is the best outside Helsinki, in the 18 surrounding municipalities in Uusimaa. It is not recommended to call this number if you are in the municipality of Helsinki and need a taxi immediately, but if you for example see a Lähitaksi taxi at a taxi stand or consider pre-ordering a taxi, it's a reliable taxi. If you for example pre-order a Lähitaksi taxi and the journey starts at a weekday afternoon, you would save

€2.40 in the base fee compared to taxis of the former Helsinki municipality monopoly.

Base fee:

- Mon through Sat from 6 am to 11 pm €3.50
- Nights from 11 pm to 6 am and public holidays €7
- Charge for waiting and slow driving 40.00 €/h

Travel fare:

- Tariff I: 1–4 persons 1.59 €/km
- Tariff II: 5–8 persons 1.91 €/km

Taksi Helsinki, +358 100 7000 for immediate orders and +358 100 0600 for pre-orders
This is the former monopoly in municipality of Helsinki. The cars can nowadays also start from other municipalities in the metropolitan area than Helsinki, but the availability is the best in the municipality of Helsinki. The cars have the 0100 7000 number in their livery. It is not recommended to call this number if you are outside the municipality of Helsinki and need a taxi

immediately, but if you for example see a Taksi Helsinki taxi at a taxi stand or consider pre-ordering a taxi, it's a reliable taxi.

Base fee:

- Mon through Fri 6 am to 8 pm, Saturdays and eves of holidays 6 am to 4 pm €5.90
- Other times €9.00
- Charge for waiting and slow driving 47.04 €/h

Travel fare:

- Fare 1: 1 to 2 people 1.60 €/km
- Fare 2: 3 to 4 people 1.91 €/km
- Fare 3: 5 to 6 people 2.07 €/km
- Fare 4: More than 6 people 2.23 €/km

Vantaan Taksi
Has the same phone number and fares as Lähitaksi for other trips than trips from the airport. For these trips the company has a HEL airport taxi brand with it's own web site http://helsinkiairporttaxi.fi/en/taxi-

services/taxi-to-airport/ and separate pricing (http://helsinkiairporttaxi.fi/en/prices/).

- ➤ Fixed fare for 1 to 4 passengers from the airport to the city center (to the zip codes 00100-00180 and 00220) € 43
- ➤ For 5 to 8 passengers €60
- ➤ Max 5 km from airport, 1–4 persons €23
- ➤ Max 5 km from airport, 5–8 persons €35

For other trips:

- ➤ 8.5 € / departure
- ➤ 1–4 passengers 1.40 € / km
- ➤ 5–8 passengers 1.90 € / km
- ➤ Charge for waiting and slow driving 0.65 € / minute (39 €/h for comparison purposes)

There are also surcharges for example pre-booking. These can be checked at the webpages of the companies. The pre-booking fare is usually about €7, so pre-book your taxi if you are travelling to the airport or otherwise need to be in your destination in a certain time. The Taksi Helsinki baggage fee is €2.80. Generally baggage that is considered large enough to warrant an extra charge is baggage that won't fit in the trunk easily, without, for example, folding down the back seat. This charge is also applied if you are travelling with a large pet - though service dogs travel free.

During weekend nights and some popular events or holidays, it can be a bit difficult to find a taxi. Walk to the nearest taxi stand or try to book by phone (2-3 EUR/call) from Taxi Helsinki +358 100 0700 , Lähitaksi +358 100 7300 or +358 100 6060 FixuTaxi. If you know in beforehand that you will need a taxi and you know the precise time, pre-order it. Call +358 100 0600 for Taxi Helsinki, otherwise the numbers are the same. A pre-order can be placed for a taxi maximum two weeks prior to the time the taxi is needed, and a minimum of a half an hour before. A pre-order fee of about €7 will be added to the taxi fare.

Drivers are not required to pick up a person hailing them on the street. If their light is on, and they pass a person hailing them, it is usually because there is a taxi stand very near by with available taxis waiting for customers. If you are not near a taxi stand, you'll very likely be able to hail a passing taxi with the light on. If the queues at night seem frustratingly long and you are willing to walk a bit, try heading towards Hakaniementori or Lauttasaari Bridge, where you can often hail a returning taxi (don't bother if the light is not on).

limos4helsinki.com is luxury and VIP taxi service. It has diverse fleet of luxurious cars, limousines, shuttles, minibuses and buses that can be used for transfers of a single or multiple number of persons.

Uber Uber is available in Helsinki region. The service is legal, if the driver has a taxi license. The car doesn't necessarily have to have a taxi livery or a taxi sign on the ceiling, a driver-specific license is enough. Some drivers don't have a required licence to operate, but there is no sanctions against customer in such a case.

By Baana
Baana - Helsinki's new "Low Line" (as opposed to NYC's High Line) opened on June 12, 2012, providing pedestrians and cyclists with a 1.3 km long connector between the Western Harbour area to Kamppi and Töölö Bay. At the Harbour end, you can also see all international cruise lines stopping to Helsinki and visit free sightseeing terrace with MiG-21BIS fighter jet on display - located at Verkkokauppa.com's electronics store. There's also a huge, 8.5 m tall Bad Bad Boy - statue located adjacent to Western Harbor and Verkkokauppa.com. On the Kamppi end, there's bicycle hire centre and cultural activities and sights.

By bike
Helsinki's City bike system was relaunched in May 2016. The system is limited to inner Helsinki, stopping at areas 4 to 7 km from the city center, and areas around certain metro stations, but tourists will typically only move in the inner area, so this won't typically

pose a problem. The registration fee is €5/day, €10/week or €25/year with the first 30 minutes of each trip included. If you do not return the bike within 30 minutes, a small fee will be debited from your cr card. If you do not return the bike within 4 hours, a large penalty fee of €80 will be debited. Be sure to find a bike rack for city bikes in time.

If you bring your own bike or rent one, you'll find an extensive network of bike routes within the city. Bikers are required by law to drive on the street next to cars unless a bike lane or integrated pedestrian/cyclists sidewalk runs next to it, and the police ticket cyclists breaking this rule. Bike lanes are clearly marked by street markings and blue traffic signs. Biking is also allowed on pedestrian streets.

Downtown bike lanes are typically on the sidewalks (instead of next to car lanes on the street) so be aware of pedestrians. Don't be afraid to ring your bell! Review your bike map carefully, as some bike routes will stop and require you to walk your bike or drive next to cars.

There is also a journey planner for cycling . Once you get out of the city centre, cycling is less complicated.

Public libraries often have free stocks of biking maps in Helsinki Metropolitan Area, so when they are not visible on tables it would be better to ask the map from the library staff.

If an ordinary bike isn't enough for you, you can also rent a cyclerickshaw (*riksa*) large enough for three from Riksavuokraus (tel. +358-50-5582525) in Eiranranta near Kaivopuisto. Prices start at €9/30 min, driver not included but available on request.

Pyöräpaja offers bicycle fixing help free of charge. True bike enthusiasts can even assemble their own bikes there. Pyöräpaja also sells bikes for quite cheap prices. (Facebook page: https://www.facebook.com/pyorapaja)

By car
Car rental is not a particularly good way of getting around Helsinki, since parking is limited and expensive. Most street-side parking in the city center is in "Zone

1" and costs €4/hour during working hours, although Saturdays (mostly) and Sundays (always) are free. There are also several large underground parking garages at Kamppi and Forum.

Seeing

Surrounded by sea and a vast archipelago, Helsinki is at its best in the summer when the dialogue between the city and nature is at its fullest. Classical Helsinki's sights can be divided into an eclectic set of churches and a wide variety of museums. For a coastal amble past some of Helsinki's minor and major sights, see the itinerary A seaside stroll in Helsinki.

If you have a short amount of time in Helsinki, you may wish to follow the recommended Helsinki itineraries, which begin at the Saarinen-designed Central Railway Station and move on to the Senate Square and the Lutheran Cathedral, the Uspenski Othrodox Cathedral, Market Square, and beyond.

Suomenlinna

If you see only one place in Helsinki in the summer, you could make it Suomenlinna . The "Gibraltar of the North" was once the greatest sea fortress in the Baltic, built by the Swedish in the mid-1700s at great expense to protect their eastern flank. But when the Russians invaded in February 1808, the bulk of the unprepared and bankrupt Swedish army hastily withdrew, allowing the Russians to conquer Helsinki without a fight and besiege the fortress. With no reinforcements in sight, commander Carl Olof Cronstedt surrendered unconditionally two months later, and Finland was ceded to the Russians. Cronstedt's actions probably saved countless civilian lives, but King Gustav IV needed a scapegoat and sentenced him to death for treason; fortunately, the losing king was himself soon overthrown, and Cronstedt lived out his years gardening.

Today's Suomenlinna is still living in its own time with only old buildings, few cars, fewer than a thousand inhabitants and lots of old fortifications, catacombs and cast iron cannons. But it's not just a museum: the sprawling complex houses restaurants, cafes, theaters and museums, and is a very popular place for a picnic on a fine summer day, watching the vast passenger ferries drift by on their way to Estonia and St Petersburg. It was included in UNESCO's World Heritage List in 1991 as a unique monument to European military architecture.

Entry to the island itself is free, but you need to pay for the ferry ride. The HSL ferry from Market Square is the cheapest and most convenient way of getting there. The ferry is a part of the Helsinki local traffic, so if you have an HSL Day Ticket it includes ferry travel. The ferry runs approximately every half hour and the trip takes about 15 minutes. You can also use the normal single-HSL tickets, you can transfer to the ferry if validated within the transfer time window. There is also a special €5, 12-hour tourist return ticket. On summer weekends the island is a popular picnic destination and you may have to wait for a long time as hundreds of people crowd the ferry terminal. In this case it may be worth it to use the more expensive private ferry company at the other end of the Market Square.

Guided tours of the island in English are available daily at 11AM, 12:30PM and 2:30PM in Jun-Aug and on Sat/Sun only at 1:30PM the rest of the year, €11/person, and history buffs will want to drop into the Suomenlinna Museum at the Visitor Centre (€7).

Other islands

A beautiful archipelago (*saaristo*) surrounds the Helsinki city center. In addition to the major islands listed below, there are scheduled services to many smaller islands, and you can also tour them by sightseeing cruise. Most of the cruises depart from the Western corner of the Market Square and last from one to several hours. Note most ferries and cruises operate only in the summer high season.

Seurasaari Open Air Museum, . A pleasant little island to the north of the center, filled with walking trails and authentic old Finnish houses collected from all over the country. An excellent half-day trip, especially in the summer, when many buildings have guides practising crafts in traditional dress. There's a very pleasant if somewhat pricy summer cafe/restaurant atop a small hill at the center of the island. Entry to the park free, entry into the museum buildings costs €9 (€6 concession), buy tickets at entrance. Take bus 24 from Erottaja at the northern end of Esplanadi to the terminus (20-30 minutes), then walk across the bridge. Beware of mercenary squirrels that will raid your bags if you carry any food.

Pihlajasaari, . Few tourists find their way here, but this is a very popular summer spot for Helsinkians, with sandy beaches (including a mixed nude beach) and a restaurant dishing out cold beer and ciders. Ferries run from Merisatama pier at the southern end of Kaivopuisto Park (tram 3B) hourly from 9:30AM to 8:30PM, 10-15 min, €5.50 return.

Korkeasaari, . An island in central Helsinki best known for Helsinki Zoo, with about 200 species of animals. Connected to the mainland by bridge (bus 16 from Central Railway Station), in summer you can also opt for a 15-min ferry ride from Hakaniemi and Market Square. Entry to the zoo €12/6 adult/child.

Vallisaari, . An old fortress island next to Suomenlinna, opened to the public in May 2016. Visitors can explore the fortifications and nature. Access by ferry from Market Square, 20-30 min (with stop at Suomenlinna on the way back), €7 return.

Parks

Esplanadi Park. Located between Market Square (Kauppatori) and the two Esplanadi boulevards, this small but stately park has a commanding position at the heart of the city. In the summer time it is full of people sitting on the lawn, meeting their friends and quite often also having a drink or two. In the summer there are often free concerts given by local artists on the stage close to Kauppatori, facing restaurant

Kappeli. If you're walking around with an ice cream or sandwich, do watch out for the aggressive birds.

Kaivopuisto. A beautiful park by the sea in the southernmost part of the city. In summer you might want to sit down for a cup of coffee in one of the seaside cafes and enjoy the view of sailboats and the people on the promenade. Housing surrounding this area is the most expensive in Helsinki.

Töölönlahti. Located northwest from the central railway station, this is a bay surrounded by a nice park that is dotted with attractions such as the Finlandia Concert Hall and the National Opera. Töölönlahti is partly in a natural state which is quite rare in major cities. Walking and jogging around the bay is a popular outdoor activity.

Sinebrychoffin puisto. Also known as "Koffin puisto", located in Punavuori district next to the Sinebrychoff art museum. Popular with young people, in the summer it is full of people having picnics or just drinking pussikalja (literally: "beer in a bag", means buying beer from a supermarket and drinking it outdoors), while in the winter kids ride sleds down the snowy slope.

Central Park (Keskuspuisto). This is a huge park starting just north of the Olympic Stadium and extending northwards for 10 km. It encompasses an area of over 1,000 hectares. The park is mostly in a natural state, with plenty of walkways, bikeways, riding paths and sports facilities including Pirkkola Sports Park (ice hockey, swimming, running) and Paloheinä (skiing, golf). A popular jogging area.

Alppipuisto . Located on the west side of the Linnanmäki amusement park, this beautiful park is a hidden gem during the summer due to the many free concerts and other events that are held there throughout the summer months.

Lauttasaari. Park on the southern tip of Lauttasaari, west of downtown Helsinki. Wooded with walking trails. You'd never know that a bustling metropolis was just a few kilometers away.

Karhupuisto. A great place to sit down and drink a few beers on a summer day. The park is located in the middle of the hip Kallio district.

Churches

If you are limited in time, the three must-see churches in Helsinki can be remembered as Red, White, and Rock. In other words, the red Uspenski Cathedral, the white Lutheran Cathedral, and the Church in the Rock.

<u>Lutheran Cathedral</u> (*Tuomiokirkko*). Aleksanterinkatu, . The unofficial symbol of the city, this striking white cathedral dominates the central Senate Square. Based on designs by Carl Ludvig Engel and completed in 1852, the cathedral has recently been refurbished and looks better than ever, with the 12 apostles on the roof once again looking down at the world below. Open daily, Sep-May 9AM-6PM, Jun-Aug 9AM-midnight. Free.

<u>The Church in the Rock</u> (*Temppeliaukion kirkko*, literally "Temple Square Church"). Lutherinkatu 3 (tram 2), . An atmospheric if minimalistic church, this church was literally dug out of solid rock. From above, it resembles a crashed UFO. The roof is made of 22 km of copper strips. Completed in 1969, this has become one of Helsinki's most popular attractions. Concerts are often held here thanks to the excellent acoustics. 10AM-5PM daily. 3€, under 18 free. Beware of busloads of obnoxious tourist groups making lots of noise even during performances. English services on Sundays at 2PM, open to the public.

<u>Uspenski Cathedral</u> (*Uspenskin katedraali*). Kanavakatu 1, . A classical onion-domed Russian church prominently located near the Market Square, Uspenski Cathedral serves Finland's small Orthodox minority and is the largest Orthodox church in Western Europe. The name comes from the Russian *uspenie*, from the Dormition (death) of the Virgin Mary. The five domes are topped with 22-carat gold, and some of the icons

within are held to be miraculous. Open Tu-F 9:30AM-4PM, Sat 9:30AM-2PM, Su 12PM-3PM. May-Sep Mon,Wed, Sat 9:30AM-4PM, Tue 9:30AM-6PM, Sun 12PM-3PM. Free.

Kamppi Chapel of silence. Kamppi, Narinkka Square. . An award-winning chapel built in 2012 that serves as ecumenical Chapel. Free.

St. John's Church (*Johanneksenkirkko*).
Korkeavuorenkatu 12. The largest church in Helsinki and a fine example of Gothic Revival architecture. M-F 12-15PM. Free.

Kallio Church (*Kallion kirkko*). On top of the hill at the end of Siltasaarenkatu. The church is built of grey granite (1912) and its massive looks dominate the view from Hakaniemi. It was designed by Finnish architect Lars Sonck. The church has both baroque and French romantic organs and concerts are organized frequently. Tu-F 12AM-6PM, Sa-Su 10AM-6PM. Free.

<u>Old Church of Helsinki</u> (*Helsingin vanha* kirkko), Lönnrotinkatu 6, and Old Church Park (Vanha kirkkopuisto). The oldest existing church in central Helsinki, designed by Carl Ludvig Engel, built between 1824 and 1826. Originally planned as a temporary building before Lutheran Cathedral would be completed in 1852, but remained in use due to the rapid population growth from the early 19th century onwards. The park is sometimes colloquially called Ruttopuisto (Plague Park) as over a thousand victims of the 1710 plague are buried next to the park. The park itself was a cemetery from the 1780s until shortly after the church's construction. Its use as a graveyard was discontinued in 1829, although some victims of the Finnish Civil War and fallen Finnish volunteers of the Estonian War of Independence were buried there in 1918 and 1919, respectively. Some 40 gravestones and memorials, as well as the Johan Sederholm's tomb remain of the cemetery.

Places of Worship

United Community Church (*UCC*). Annankatu 7, . International, bible-based and nondenominational church that welcomes both Finns and foreigners to attend. Services in Helsinki and Espoo on Sundays. Free.

Museums and galleries

Many of Helsinki's museums are as interesting from the outside as from the inside. Architecture buffs will get a kick out of Helsinki's Neo-Classical center, centered around Senate Square (*Senaatintori*), where a statue of the liberal Russian czar Alexander II stands guard. Aleksanterinkatu and the Railway Station square also have some beautiful neo-classical buildings look out for the Romantic Kalevala-esque themes but unfortunately these areas also have many concrete monstrosities mixed in.

Ateneum Art Museum, Kaivokatu 2, +358 294 500 500 (), . Open Tue&Fri 10AM-6PM, Wed&Thu 10AM-8PM, Sat&Sun 10AM-5PM. Closed on Mondays. Ateneum can be considered the most nationally significant art museum, and it has the largest collection of paintings and sculptures in Finland. Particularly notable is the collection of works by major Finnish artists. Works include renowned interpretations of the national epic Kalevala. Adults 15€, discount admission 13€, under 18 year-olds free..

Design Museum, Korkeavuorenkatu 23, +358 9 622 0540, . Open Tu 11AM-8PM, W-Su 11AM-6PM. Closed Mondays.. Exhibitions of modern commercial and industrial design and modern art. The permanent exhibit in the basement showcases the history of consumer-goods design over the course of the 20th century, with a particular focus on the contributions of Finnish designers. €10 for adults, €3 for students, and free for children.

Helsinki City Museum, Sofiankatu 4, +358 9 3103 6630, . The museum actually covers a whole series of old buildings around Helsinki, but the centerpiece is the (short) street of Sofiankatu itself, carefully restored as a replica of the 1930s. Free.

Kiasma Museum of Contemporary Art, Mannerheiminaukio 2, +358 294 500 501 (fax: +358 294 500 575), . Tue 10AM-5PM, Wed-Fri 10AM-8.30PM, Sat 10AM-6PM, Sun 10AM-5PM. Closed on Mondays.. The sometimes unusual collections mostly include works by contemporary Finnish artists and artists from nearby countries. There are also periodical exhibitions. The building itself is arguably a work of art. Adults 14€, discount admission 12€, under 18 year-olds for free. First Friday of the month is free for everyone.

The National Museum of Finland (*Kansallismuseo*), Mannerheimintie 34, +358 295 33 6901, . Tue-Sun 11-18, Mon closed. A beautiful classical building houses this old museum, which has recently been renovated. National Museum illustrates Finnish history from prehistoric times to the present. Major archaeological finds. Temporary exhibitions. Embark a time-trip through the history of Finland. The museum's unique exhibits tells of the life from a period of over 10,000 years. 0-10€ Free admission on Friday from 4 p.m. till 6 p.m..

Museum of Cultures (*Kulttuurien museo*),

Mannerheimintie 34, Helsinki, . Tue-Sun 11-18, Mon closed. The exhibitions provide perspectives into both past and present and the everyday life of peoples throughout the world, as well as in multicultural Finland. The aim of the exhibitions is to provide alternative ways of reviewing the development of the world and also to remind of the existence of small, nearly extinct or repressed peoples and groups. The Museum of Cultures is closed in Tennis Palace and will move to the National Museum's premises in 2013 - with a new exhibition on the world's religions scheduled for spring 2014. 0-9€ Free admission on Friday from 4 p.m. till 6 p.m..

Museum of Finnish Architecture, Kasarmikatu 24, +358 9 8567 5100, . Open Tue-Sun 11AM-6PM, Wed 11AM-8PM. Closed Mondays.. Changing exhibitions on

Finnish and international architecture. Permanent exhibition on 20th century Finnish architecture. Bookshop and Library.

Gallery Forum Box, Ruoholahdenranta 3 a, . Tue-Fri 11AM-5PM, Sat-Sun 12PM-5PM. A Contemporary Art Gallery, changing exhibitions and cultural events.

Heureka Science Centre, Tikkurila (*near Tikkurila train station*), . M-W, Th 10AM-8PM, F 10AM-5PM, Sa-Su 10AM-6PM.. If you have children, this is a great place for a day trip. Hands-on science tests and exhibitions plus Verne super-cinema. There's also a Heureka Shop, where you can buy interesting science-related memorabilia. Adult: €21; Children (6-15): €14.

Mannerheim Museum, Kalliolinnantie 14 (*Trams 2 and 3*), . Fri, Sat, Su 11AM-4PM. Finnish Marshall Carl Gustav Emil Mannerheim lived in this villa 1924—51. The museum contains his personal home and his vast array of items acquired during his life and on his long travels. €8.

Military Museum, Maurinkatu 1 (*Trams 7A and 7B*), . Tu-Th 11AM–5PM, F–Su 11AM–4PM. Closed Mondays.. Founded in 1929, the central museum of the Finnish Defence Forces. €4.

Military Museum Manege, Suomenlinna, Iso Mustasaari (*Take an inexpensive ferry from Kauppatori*), . Open summertime (12.5-31.8, closed 19-21.6) daily 11AM–6PM. Exhibits vehicles and armament used by Finnish forces during Winter War and WW2. €5.

Submarine Vesikko, Suomenlinna, Susisaari (*Take an inexpensive ferry from Kauppatori*), . Open summertime (12.5-31.8, closed 19-21.6) daily 11AM–6PM. Vesikko was one of five submarines to serve the Finnish Navy during the wars in 1939-44. It´s also the only surviving German Type II (Vesikko was the prototype) submarine in the world. €5.

Olympic sights

Helsinki is an Olympic city, the host of the 1952 Olympic Games.

<u>Olympic Stadium</u>, . Originally built for the Olympics of 1940 (cancelled due to WW II) and renovated for the 2005 World Athletic Championships. Next to the stadium are soccer fields. There is Museum of Sport in the stadium building. Another stadium called Sonera stadium is not far from the Olympic site. The most popular building in the complex, though, is the Uimastadion, Helsinki's largest outdoor pool (open May-Sep), whose three pools and water slides draw around 5,000 visitors a day in the summer. After the war, the pool was used to store herring and potatoes. The olympic stadium will be closed from 2015 until year 2019, due to construction and modernisation work

<u>Olympic Tower</u>. The stadium features 72m high tower (14 storeys) that offers a great view over the city. The tower will be closed from 2015 until year 2019, due to construction and modernisation work

Other

Parliament House (*Eduskunta*), Mannerheimintie 30, . The House of the 200-seat Parliament of Finland was designed by J.S. Sirén in the classic style of the 1920s and officially inaugurated in 1931. The interior is classical with a touch of functionalism and art deco. Tours in English at 11AM and 12PM on Sat, 12PM and 1PM on Sun. During the months of Jul and Aug English tours are at 1PM on weekdays (and not available on weekends). Free. *Under extensive renovation 2007–2017*

Finlandia Hall, Mannerheimintie 13, . Designed by Finland's best known architect Alvar Aalto and located across the street from the National Museum, the marble Finlandia Hall is a popular congress and concert venue in Helsinki. The building itself is worth a visit particularly for architecture buffs, with guided tours available (€6/4. Be sure to view the building also from across the Töölönlahti bay in the evening when it is floodlit. M-F 9AM-4PM. Free.

Sibelius Monument, Sibelius Park, . The world-famous composer Jean Sibelius' monument was designed by sculptress Eila Hiltunen and unveiled in 1967. It is one of the best-known tourist attractions in Helsinki as nearly every guided tourist tour is brought to Sibelius Park to marvel at this unique work of art resembling organ pipes, welded together from 600 pipes and weighing over 24 metric tons.

Korjaamo Cultural Factory, Töölönkatu 51 +358 400 824 229 Situated in the old tram depot, Korjaamo is made up of galleries, a café, bar, club space, a theatre, shop, and even the Tram Museum is still here. Since the Vaunuhalli was opened in the summer of 2008, Korjaamo is now the biggest cultural centre in the country. While the work is diverse, you could say that the kind of art on offer at Korjaamo is independent, different, and worth keeping an eye on.

Tropicario Sturenkatu 27. An indoors snakes + lizards exhibition, with a large collection of large and small snakes, including pythons, anacondas, black mambas, and a number of species of reptiles, including crocodiles and iguanas. No Finnish snakes or lizards! Accessible by tram 7 and some bus lines from the city center in about 30 minutes. Admission adults 14 euros children 8 euros. Open daily from 10am to 6pm.

Doing

<u>Vintage tram ride</u>, Havis Amanda fountain at Market square, . Sat-Sun 10 am - 5 pm. Enjoy a ride on a century-old tram! If the weather is warm, sit in the open trailer car. The driver takes you on a 20-minute loop tour around the city centre area (there is no commentary but photo opportunities are plenty due to there being no windows in the open tram from 1909!). The service operates annually from mid-May to the end of August, Saturdays and Sundays only, with departures from the Market Square half-hourly between 10 and 5. €5.

<u>Winter World Helsinki</u>, Savikiekontie 4, 00940 helsinki, . 10:00-14:00. Unique Lapland has brought the wonderful Lapland winter into the city of Helsinki.

Snow attractions and activities are available in any weather: igloos, ice sculptures, sliding hill, kick-sledding and tandem skiing. Everything is built indoors using snow and ice. The weather forecast of the day is always -3 degrees Celsius, no wind, steady weather conditions. During summer season open 10:00-14:00 daily. www.winterworld.fi

Ice pool It is a Finnish custom of doing a sauna and then jumping into ice cold water. Be warned, it is freezing, even if you only go in for a few seconds. Please consider the health risks before swimming.

Amusement parks

Linnanmäki . (*Trams 3 and 8, or bus 23*) The oldest amusement park in Finland, famous for its wooden roller coaster. Entrance to the park is free of charge, all-day passes €38 (same for children and adults). Tickets for individual rides €8. There are about 10 free rides for small children up to about 4 or 5 years old. Open only during the summer, however the adjacent

Sea Life aquarium at Tivolikuja 1 is open throughout the year.

<u>Serena Water Amusement Park</u> , Tornimäentie 10, Espoo (*Bus 339 from Helsinki Bus Station*), tel. *+358 9 8870550*. "" Open 11AM-8PM daily. This is the largest water park in the Nordic countries with some 2,000 sq.m. of heated pools indoors. The buildings have seen their best days, but kids love the water slides. An extra 1,000 m² of outdoor area is open in the summer. Serena is at its best in winter when you can kick back in a jacuzzi and watch people ski on the other side of the glass windows. All-day pass €24,5 (bought online €23,5), evening ticket €20,5 (16:00-20:00 only), family ticket (2 adults, 2 children) €94 (online €90), 2 adults+3 children €117,5 (online €112,25).

<u>Flamingo Entertainment Center</u> , Tasetie 8, Vantaa. (*Buses 615, 614 and 451 from Helsinki Railway Station or bus 562 from Tikkurila Station*) A big entertainment complex located near the airport in Vantaa, next to a large shopping mall Jumbo, just north of Helsinki.

Biggest attractions are <u>Flamingo Spa & Wellness</u> with pretty cool and fast slides in the water park section and a large selection of relaxation pools, jacuzzis and different saunas in the other section, and <u>Hohtogolf West Coast</u> which is a glow in the dark 15-hole miniature golf course with over-the-top mechanized special effects and a special "horror" section. Cheesy but fun, especially after a few drinks from the bar. Other attractions in Flamingo include a small casino, a 3D movie theater, many pubs and restaurants, a variety of specialist shops, a large hotel and one of the biggest nightclubs in Finland.

<u>Hoplop activity hall for kids</u> , large indoor playgrounds for children, with several locations. Slides, climbing, et cetera.

- ➢ Ruoholahti, -5th undergound floor in the shopping mall complex at Ruoholahti metro station
- ➢ Mankkaa (part of the Espoo/Mankkaa sports park, close to the Niittykumpu metro station

> Savikiekontie 4, Helsinki. (*Buses 519 and 54 from Itäkeskus metro station*)

Cinema

In downtown Helsinki, there are two large multiplexes: Tennispalatsi located in Salomonkatu 15, Kamppi and Kinopalatsi in Kaisaniemenkatu 2, Kaisaniemi, both maintained by Finnkino, the largest movie theater chain in Finland. In addition, Finnkino operated a historic cinema with two screens, Maxim, in Kluuvikatu 1, Kluuvi. Maxim has been closed for renovation since January 2016.

Theaters concentrating on classic and art house films are few and far between in Helsinki today. The art deco theater Orion, Eerikinkatu 15, run by the Finnish National Audiovisual Institute, screens a wide variety of films, including classics. Tickets 6,50€ for non-members and 6€ with a membership card. Kino Engel, Sofiankatu 4 near Senaatintori, focuses on European and world cinema. Tickets 9€. In Summer, also Kesäkino (Summer Cinema) is held in the courtyard of Café Engel,

Aleksanterinkatu 26. Tickets (12€) can be bought from the Kino Engel counter and for the same night also from the Kesäkino door 45 minutes before the screening. Kesäkino will operate also in Summer 2016 in spite of the Kino Engel renovation. New movie theaters in town include Kino Sheryl in Arabianranta and Korjaamo Kino in Töölö. Kino Sheryl is owned by a student organization TOKYO ry of Aalto University's School of Arts, Design and Architechture. Tickets are €8 on weekdays and €10 on weekends, holidays and for premieres. Korjaamo Kino screens selected premieres, quality independent films and audience favourites. Tickets €11.

There are also some (small) independent movie theaters in neighboring Espoo, Vantaa and Kauniainen showing mainly the bigger blockbusters: Bio Grand in Tikkurila, Vantaa, Bio Jaseka in Myyrmäki, Vantaa, Bio Grani in Kauniainen and Kino Tapiola in Tapiola, Espoo. Many of them have a matinée series of cheaper, more art house screenings supported by the local culture board. In addition, Finnkino operates three screens in Omenacinema in the Iso Omena shopping center in Matinkylä, Espoo as well as six screens in Flamingo multiplex in the entertainment center Flamingo in Vantaa. In Leppävaara, Espoo there are also six screens in the Sello multiplex at the Sello shopping center.

Luckily, several film festivals enrich the cinema culture in Helsinki region. The biggest is the Helsinki International Film Festival - Love and Anarchy held annually in September. Espoo has its own international film festival Espoo Ciné held every August in Tapiola and Leppävaara. In January, Helsinki Documentary Film Festival Docpoint takes over. Some of the smaller film festivals include (to name few) Lens Politica showing political films and art, Season Film Festival concentrating on films of and by women, and Night Visions focusing on horror, fantasy, science fiction, action and cult cinema. Cinemania site collects at least some of the festivals together.

Most films in Finland are shown in the original language with Finnish and Swedish subtitles. The only exception is children's films (usually animations) which might be dubbed in Finnish.

Concerts

Helsinki has an active cultural life and tickets are generally inexpensive. Important performing groups include:

National Opera (Kansallisooppera), Helsinginkatu 58, tel. +358-9-403021, . Lavishly subsidized, but it's still easy to get good seats. Tickets €14-84. Students can buy discount tickets for performances on the same day for 10 euros if there are still seats left, but these tickets have to be bought in person. An international student card is valid. Pensioners get 5 euros off, and children get their tickets at half regular price. Also runs the National Ballet (Kansallisbaletti).

Helsinki Philharmonic Orchestra (Kaupunginorkesteri), . Performances have recently moved to the Music

House, a brand new visually questionable but acustically excellent concert hall. Tickets €20. On selected Wednesdays you can go see dress rehearsals for as little as 3 euros per person. The rehearsals start 9.30 AM. Check availability on the site before showing up at the Music House!

UMO Jazz Orchestra, . An important part of Finnish jazz life, known for performing new Finnish music alongside interesting shows, such as with new circus. Various venues.

Festivals

Helsinki's celebrations are among the most exciting in the country.

Lux Helsinki, beginning of January. Lux Helsinki is an annual event comprising of light installations to cheer residents' and visitors' minds during the darkest time of the year. They are on display over several nights. Lux Helsinki can also be enjoyed as part of a guided walking tour.

Vappu (Walpurgis Night), Apr 30-May 1. Originally a north European pagan carnival, Vappu is an excuse for students to wear brightly colored overalls and for everybody to drink vast amounts of alcohol. At 6PM on Apr 30, the statue of Havis Amanda at the Market Square is crowned with a student's cap and the revelry begins in the streets. Things can get a little ugly outside as the night wears on, so it's wiser to head indoors to the bars, clubs and restaurants, all of which have massive Vappu parties. The following morning, the party heads to the Kaivopuisto park for a champagne picnic, regardless of the weather. If the weather is good, up to 70,000 people will show up. Left-wing parties hold rallies and speeches (Labor Day, May 1), but the event is increasingly non-political.

Helsinki-päivä (Helsinki Day), Jun 12. This is the birthday of the city. It traditionally starts with the mayor's morning coffee and is celebrated throughout the day with a variety of concerts, performances, exhibitions and guided tours around the city.

Juhannus (Midsummer Festival), Friday between Jun 19 and Jun 25. Although a large bonfire is lit in Seurasaari, the celebration is low key as the tradition is to celebrate "the nightless night" at summer cottages in the countryside. Although some celebrate Juhannus in Helsinki as well, the streets are often eerily empty and the doors of the shops closed.

Tuska Open Air, . An annual, 3-day heavy metal festival, featuring acts from all over the world, held in June.

Crystal Fair, . A July convention of the Bronies, fans of Little Pony: Friendship is Magic.

Flow Festival, . Annual 3-day urban and electronic music festival, held in mid-August at Suvilahti. Noted for its high-end arrangements marrying music to design and gourmet food, Flow has expanded to include installations, arts and workshops in the past few years.

Taiteiden Yö (Night of the Arts), near the end of Aug. The peak of the multi-week Helsinki Festival , called "little vappu" by many as the streets are full of revelers. The official event is marked by performing arts through the night. The Night of the Arts was originally organized by local bookstores in the 1990s. It's now organized by the city. During the last few years, the event has slightly returned to its origin as an arts and culture event.

Helsinki International Film Festival, . Also known as Rakkautta & Anarkiaa (Love & Anarchy) and held annually in September, HIFF features a wide selection of films from all over the world. Asian films have been a special focus in the history of the festival that is celebrating its 25th anniversary in 2012.

Joulu (Christmas). In the weeks before Christmas, Aleksanterinkatu is festively lit up (starting on the last Sunday of November) and the Esplanadi hosts an open-air Christmas market. But Christmas itself is a family event, so on the 24th, everything shuts down and stays closed until December 26th.

Outdoors

Hietaniemi Beach, Hietaniemenkatu. It's safe to say that most people don't come to Helsinki for the beaches, but on a hot summer day *Hietsu* (as it is known among the locals) is a good place to be. Beach volleyball, swimming and various events are popular. Buses 24 and 18 or tram 2 from Kamppi/Rautatientori, or just walk (15-20 min from the centre).

Aurinkolahti Beach, Solvikinkatu, Vuosaari. Spacier and calmer than Hietsu, the Aurinkolahti Beach is frequented by everyone from youth to families. It is located in the neighbourhood of Vuosaari. 700 m walk or bus 90 towards "Vuosaaren satama" (stops "Ivan Fallinin kuja" and "G. Pauligin katu") from the Metro station Vuosaari (20min from the centre).

Härmälä Farm, Mäntykummuntie 6, Vantaa, tel. *+358 9 876 7339, +358 (0)400 880 539. (Bus 717 from Helsinki Railway Station)* Open by arrangement all year. A typical Finnish farm located in the village of Sotunki in eastern Vantaa and surrounded by a picturesque landscape. On the farm you can meet animals representing the traditional Finnish stock: cows, sheep, goats, pigs, horses and more. Admission €3, families €10.

<u>Fallkulla Farm</u>, Malminkaari 24, Helsinki. Farm with cows, pigs, goats, chicken, rabbits and horses. Open year round from Wednesday to Friday 10am to 6pm, Sundays 10am to 3pm. Accessible from city center by local train in less than 40 minutes (750 meter walk from train stop Tapanila.) Run by the city of Helsinki. Free admission.

<u>Haltiala Farm</u>, Laamannintie 17, Helsinki. Farm with cows, sheep, pigs, chicken. Open year round, usually weekdays 6pm to 8pm, weekends 11am to 6pm (check before going!) Run by the City of Helsinki. From city center 45 to 55 minutes by buses 614 or 615 and 1 km walk. Free admission.

<u>Feel the nature treks</u>, tel. +358 10 581 3890. Feel the nature organizes outdoor activities around Helsinki region. Snowshoes, canoes, seakayaks, hiking, skiing

including all equipment needed and transport from Helsinki centre. Scheduled trips for individuals also.

At Sea

Helsinki is located at the Finnish Gulf, and several cruise liners arrange trips out to the archipelago ranging from short hops lasting only an hour or two to trips ranging a full day.

Söderskär Lighthouse, (*Royal Line from Kauppatori market*), +358 400 502 771 (), . Boat at 11AM on Tue, Thu, Sat (29.6.-14.8.2010). An old secluded lighthouse island out at the sea, in the middle of a bird reservoir. Day trips are arranged by Royal Line , including a lunch, a guided tour of the lighthouse (Finnish/English) and a couple hours time to linger at the island, but it is also possible to stay at the island for the night. Day cruise €53/25, hostel starting at €40/person.

Skippered Day Sailing, Laivastokatu 1, Katajanokka, +358-50-592 91 41 (), . leaves daily 10AM. Visit the coastal archipelago on a 35ft sailboat, for two hours or full day trips with an experienced skipper. Island hopping is also possible. from €60.

Tailored Boat Trips, Merisatama, +358505285584, . See the beautiful Helsinki archipelago with a private boat and captain. It's possible to arrange tailored boat trips for up to 6 person. Captain has a good knowledge about the nice places that are worth to visit. Trips can be started from any sea harbour in Helsinki.

Saunas

Arlan sauna (also known as Sauna Arla) , Kaarlenkatu 15, . Old public sauna in Kallio. Separate saunas for men and women. Washing service and traditional bloodletting (*kuppaus*) also available. €12 for adults, students €10.

Kotiharjun sauna , Harjutorinkatu 1. This is the last wood burning public sauna in Helsinki. Separate saunas for men and women. There's a good chance you'll find a top level chess match in the dressing room. Don't miss cooling off outside, especially in winter. On

Saturdays you'll find bachelor partiers (Kotiharju is pretty near to Kallio's nightlife). €12 for adults, students & pensioners €8.5, towel €3 extra.

<u>Sauna Hermanni</u>, Hämeentie 63, . Founded in 1953 and recently renovated in that style (with some added flair), Hermanni is an excellent public sauna. It has an electric heater an awesome massive cage holding 300kg rocks. Really fun to pour water on. Small tunnelesque room creates powerful löyly (steam). Soft drinks and snacks available. Separate saunas for men and women. Relax in change room or outside at garden table. There's a hammock near the table use it if you can. Very easy to reach with tram 6 or 8, the stop (Hauhon puisto) is right outside. Open from Monday to Saturday so it's your best option on a Monday. Mon-Fri 3-8pm, Sat 2-7pm. Sauna is open for bathing one hour past closing time. €10 for adults, students €8.

<u>Yrjönkadun Uimahalli</u>, Yrjönkatu 21b in Helsinki, across from the Torni Hotel, an art-deco bath house with three types of saunas and a swimming pool. Take a

sauna and swim in the nude. There are separate days for women and men. Bathing suits are not banned, but almost everyone goes without one. Men's swimming days are: Tuesday, Thursday, Saturday; Women's days: Monday, Wednesday, Friday, Sunday. 1st Floor €5.00 (or €5.40 with a lockable stall or 'cabin'), 2nd Floor €14. The second floor includes access to a steam sauna and a wood-heated sauna, as well as a café.

Kämp Spa, Kluuvikatu 4 B, (Kämp Gallery 8th floor), +358 9 5761 1330 (), . Mon–Fri 9am - 8pm, Sat 9am - 8pm, Sun 9am - 1pm and 4pm - 8pm (gym and sauna area). Kämp Spa is located in the heart of Helsinki. In addition to the spa treatments, the Spa counts with a gym and 3 different saunas.

Kuusijärvi, Kuusijärventie 3, Vantaa, . This traditional smoke sauna is located in Vantaa but very easy to reach from Helsinki Railway Station. Situated in Kuusijärvi Outdoor Centre and besides a beautiful lake, it's widely regarded as one of the best traditional saunas in the capital region. Rebuilt in 2011. €10 for adults, students/children €6. Take your swim gear with you, as the smoke sauna is mixed-sex. Kuusijärvi is one of the rare places in Helsinki area where winter swimming is possible for public every day during the winter season.

Kaurilan Sauna, Heikinniementie 9, Helsinki. Authentic Finnish wood-heated sauna in a 19th century sauna building, located in middle of nature, just 15 min bus ride from Helsinki city center. Relax in front of fireplace in changing room or outside in a peaceful garden. 2 hour public shifts are during Mon, Tue and Wed evenings (men, women and mixed shifts are available). The sauna is operated by a family living in the same courtyard. Pre-booking is required, ticket (€16) includes hand-made hemp fabric towels, sauna seat covers as well as washing products.

Sompasauna, The most interesting super public Sauna close to Kalasatama metro station. Highly recommended.

Sports

<u>Salmisaaren Liikuntakeskus</u>, Energiakatu 3 (*next to Helsinki Energia @ Ruoholahti*), . New sports mall in Helsinki, includes indoor beach, bowling, ice hockey, wall climbing, gym, restaurant and lots more...

<u>Sonera Stadium</u>, Urheilukatu 5 (*next to Olympic Stadium*), . The home of football (soccer) team HJK . Tickets for matches start from €12. *Name changed from Finnair Stadium in August 2010 due to corporate sponsorship change*

<u>Hartwall Areena</u>, Areenankuja 1 (*7 min walk from Pasila station, 10 min walk from Tram 7 stop at Kyllikinportti*), . The largest indoor arena in Finland, the home of ice hockey team *Jokerit* and also a popular venue for concerts.

<u>Natura Viva - Vuosaari Paddling Center</u>, Ramsinniementie 14, +358503768585, . Vuosaari Paddling Center is the leading organizer of kayaking activities in the Helsinki region. The kayak rental is

open from the beginning of June until the end of August every day. In May and September on demand. Guided tours, trips and courses are also possible. Rentals start at 14 € per 2 hours.

<u>Outdoor Icepark skating in winter</u>, Railway Station Square (*in the center of Helsinki*), . A pair of skates can be rented for an additional fee. The connected Café offers the opportunity of defrosting with a cup of hot glögi. There are also dozens of other places to go skating in Helsinki, including natural and indoor skating rinks. Their list is available from the the Helsinki City web .

Buying

Shopping in Helsinki is generally expensive, but fans of Finnish and Nordic design will find plenty of things of interest. From the beginning of 2016, the shopping hours have been freed from regulation, meaning that each shop can decide for themselves. Thus the opening hours should be checked in advance as there is and will be more and more variation. Most large shops and department stores have been open weekdays from 9AM to 9PM. As in the rest of Finland, most shops close by 6PM on Saturday and Sunday (as of 2010 all shops are allowed to open every Sunday between noon and 6PM). A notable exception is the Asematunneli complex, located underground adjacent to the Central Railway Station, most shops here are open until 10PM almost every day of the year.

Grocery stores K-Supermarket and Lidl in the Kamppi Center (see below) and the S-Market supermarket below Sokos, next to the railway station, are open every day until 10PM. Small grocery stores and the R-Kioski convenience store chain are open till 10PM or 11PM year-round, too. A handful of small Alepa grocery stores are open 24 hours a day except on national holidays, including Alepa Eliel, located under the commuter train tracks at the Central Railway Station. In the centre you will find small Delish and Pick A Deli convenience stores in the city center, open 24 hours a day year round but more expensive than regular grocery stores.

Department stores and shopping malls
Helsinki's main shopping street is Aleksanterinkatu (*Aleksi*), which runs from Senate Square to Mannerheimintie. On Aleksi you can find plenty of shops and the largest department store in Scandinavia, Stockmann. The parallel Esplanadi boulevards have expensive specialty boutiques. The only store by an international luxury brand in Finland is on Esplanadi: Louis Vuitton. Access to the area is easy, as trams 3, 4/4T and 7A/7B all run down Aleksanterinkatu, and the area is just a stone's throw from the Central Railway Station and Helsingin yliopisto metro stations. Close by, in the Kamppi area, you can find the shopping centres Kamppi and Forum and the department store Sokos. Large shopping malls can be found in the suburbs and accessed by public transport from the Central Railway Station.

<u>Academic Bookstore</u> (*Akateeminen Kirjakauppa*). Keskuskatu (*opposite Stockmann*), . The largest bookstore in Northern Europe, with extensive selections in English too. An underground passage connects the bookstore to Stockmann. If for no other reason the bookstore's architechture (Alvar Aalto) and pleasant second floor cafeteria (one of the few with table service in Helsinki) might be enough reason to visit. Tram: 3, 4, 6, 7, 9, 10.

<u>Stockmann</u>. Corner of Aleksanterinkatu and Mannerheimintie, . The flagship of Finland's premier department store chain. When locals meet "under the clock" (*kellon alla*), they mean the one under the Aleksanterinkatu entrance to Stockmann. A large selection of souvenirs and Finnish goods serve tourists on one of the top floors. he Herkku supermarket in the basement offers an amazing range of gourmet food. There are also smaller branches of Stockmann at the malls of Itäkeskus, Jumbo, Tapiola and the airport. Tram: 2, 3, 4, 6, 7, 9, 10.

Itis. . The largest shopping mall in the Nordic countries with some 240 shops. Comes with an unexpected African and Middle Eastern vibe due to the high number of immigrants residing in the adjacent neighbourhoods, who spend free time there with friends and family. Metro: Itäkeskus, about 16 minutes from the center.

Galleria Esplanad, between Mikonkatu and Kluuvikatu, . Helsinki's fanciest shopping mall, with local brands like Marimekko, Aarikka and Iittala. Tram: 3, 4, 6, 7, 9. Metro: Helsingin yliopisto.

Kamppi Center (*Kampin Keskus*), . Big shopping mall in the center of Helsinki. Plenty of stores and restaurants. Long-distance bus terminal in the basement. Metro: Kamppi.

Kluuvi. Aleksanterinkatu 9. Re-opened after extensive renovations in Autumn 2011, the Kluuvi shopping centre features a wide range of small stores. Perhaps the most interesting concept is the Eat & Joy Markethall selling organic and local food in the basement. Grind your own flour and fill your bottles with crude milk but be prepared for steep prices. Tram: 2, 3, 4, 6, 7, 9. Metro: Helsingin yliopisto.

<u>Kauppakeskus Ruoholahti</u>. . The "suburban" shopping mall closest to the center. Metro: Ruoholahti. Tram: 8.

<u>Sokos</u>. . A large department store located right next to the railway station. Tram: 2, 3, 4, 6, 7, 9, 10, Metro: Central Railway Station.

<u>Citycenter</u>, Kaivokatu 8, . Tram: 2, 3, 4, 6, 7, 9, 10, Metro: Central Railway Station

<u>Verkkokauppa.com</u>. . Northern Europe's and probably also Europe's largest home-electronics store with 20 000 m2 of retail space. The best spot for electronics, computers, digital cameras, mobile phones, etc. in Helsinki (but you are usually better off internet-shopping from Germany). Located 2 km from the Helsinki city center. Store also features Finland's largest and free sightseeing terrace with a MiG-21BIS fighter plane. Free parking for 2 hours. Metro:

Ruoholahti. Tram: 9 and 6T take you door-to-door from the railway station. Also terminal to Tallinn, Estonia and St. Petersburg, Russia is one the other side of the street looking from Verkkokauppa.com

In the suburbs of Vantaa and Espoo you can also find big shopping malls. Vantaa has Jumbo(including Flamingo) and Myyrmanni , while Espoo has Iso Omena and Sello . All of these are easily accessible by public transport or by car (free parking), but don't provide anything that would not be available in the city center.

Design
There are high-end design stores around Aleksanterinkatu and Etelä-Esplanadi. The Design District Helsinki area around Uudenmaankatu and Iso Roobertinkatu is full of design and antique shops, fashion stores, museums, art galleries, restaurants and showrooms. Here you can find the most interesting names, classics, trend-setters and so much more. Visit

Design Forum Finland at Erottajankatu 7 to get a map of shops and galleries.

<u>Aero</u>, Yrjönkatu 8, . New and vintage design furniture, lighting, textiles, jewelery, glass. Finnish designers represented include Eero Aarnio, Alvar Aalto, Tapio Wirkkala, Timo Sarpaneva and Ilmari Tapiovaara. Not for the budget traveller.

<u>Arabia Factory Shop</u>. Hämeentie 135 (*Tram 6 & 8 terminus*), . Factory outlet for Arabia ceramics and Iittala glassware, best known for selling slightly defective goods at modestly discounted prices. Open M-F 10AM-8PM, Sa-Su 10AM-4PM.

<u>Helsinki 10</u>, Eerikinkatu 3, tel. *+358*-10-5489801, . This bright-white "lifestyle department store" sells both international and Finnish (designer) labels such as Raf Simons, Wood Wood, Acne and April77 as well as second-hand clothes, accessories, records, magazines etc. Open M-F 11AM-8PM, Sa 11AM-6PM.

Iittala Shop, Pohjoisesplanadi 25, . An airy concept store for the Iittala brand of Finnish glassware, pans, kitchen utensils and more. Personal service by the friendly staff. Open M-F 10AM-7PM, Sa 10AM-4PM.

Ivana Helsinki, Uudenmaankatu 15, tel. *+358 9* 6224422, . Internationally recognized designer clothes, handmade in Finland.

Marimekko. Pohjoisesplanadi 33, tel. *+358 9* 686 0240, . Innovative and unique Finnish interior design, bags, and fabrics. This is the flagship store, but items can also be found at the Kämp Gallery, Kamppi Centre, Hakaniemi Market Hall, or their factory shop (Kirvesmiehenkatu 7, tel. *+358 9*758 7244).

Myymälä2, Uudenmaankatu 23, . Gallery and shop for young designers, artists and musicians. And while you are there, check out Lux shop on the opposite side of the street.

Paloni, Eerikinkatu 7, tel. +358-50-5894131, . Paloni is a creative design concept store. It sells items that are designed and made by over 70 independent designers. Paloni's product range covers women's clothing, accessories, jewellery, home decor, gift items and children's clothing. Open M-F 11AM-7PM, Sa 11AM-4PM.

TRE, Mikonkatu 6, tel. +358-29-1700-430, . TRE is the world's largest Finnish design and fashion store. Wide range of design, furniture, lifestyle products, organic cosmetics and fashion. The vegetarian cafe Cargo in the back is also worth a visit. Open M-F 11AM-7PM, Sa 11AM-6PM.

Markets
Most outdoor markets in Helsinki are open only in summer, but the market halls are open all year round. They are great places to taste Finnish delicacies.

Hakaniemi Market Hall (Hakaniemen kauppahalli) and Hakaniemi Open-Air Market (Hakaniemen tori). A busy market frequented by locals, this is where you can find specialities at affordable prices. The first floor of the market hall is largely food. Head to the second floor for handicrafts and souvenirs. The open-air market offers fresh vegetables and seasonal products. Walking up Hämeentie from Hakaniemi market, you'll find most of Helsinki's African, Middle Eastern, Indian and Asian grocery stores. Metro: Hakaniemi. Tram: 1, 1A, 3, 6, 6T, 7, 9.

Hietalahti Market Hall , Hietalahdentori (tram 6), tel. +358 9 670145. Broad variety of fresh foods and preserved foods to take as souvenir. You can have a quick snack, or enjoy lunch or dinner at the popular restaurants and cafés at the hall. From city center a nice 10min walk at the opposite end of Bulevardi street. Open Mon-Tue 8am-6pm & Wed-Sat 8am-10pm.

Hietalahti Open Air Flea market. Next to Hietalahti Restaurant Hall, this is the most popular flea market in Helsinki. Open year round, but busiest from May to August.

Market Square (Kauppatori). At the end of Esplanadi facing the sea, and just a block from the Lutheran

Cathedral or the Uspenski Cathedral, this open-air market square is in the must-see zone for most visitors and sells fresh fish and produce from all over Finland. Open year round. It's busiest in summer, although the Christmas Market in December is also worth a look. One section of the market is devoted to souvenirs, but best buys here are the fresh berries and other produce. In summer, try the sweet green peas (herne). Just pop open the pod and eat as is. Market Square is also the site of the Havis Amanda fountain.

Old Market Hall (Vanha kauppahalli), . Just south of Market Square, this renovated old brick building houses Finland's best collection of gourmet food boutiques. Try to find the stall which sells bear salami! Tram: 2, 3, 1, 1A.

Eating

Helsinki has by far the best cosmopolitan restaurants in Finland, and is a good place to escape the usual diet of meat and potatoes. As usual in Finland the best time to eat out is **lunch**, when most restaurants offer lunch specials for around €10. Lunch are typically served from 10:30AM to 2PM, but the times vary.

A surprisingly large number of restaurants close down for a month or more in summer (July-August), so call ahead to avoid disappointment.

Budget
Budget choices are largely limited to fast food, although there are a couple of workaday Finnish eateries in the mix. In addition to McDonald's and its Finnish imitators Hesburger/Carrols, Helsinki is also full of pizza and kebab places, where a meal typically costs around €7-8 (sometimes as low as €4-5, especially in Kallio). A more healthy option is Unicafe , a chain of restaurants owned by the Helsinki University student union, which has around 10 outlets in central Helsinki and offers full meals from €5.70, including vegetarian options..

Fat Ramen, Lönnrotinkatu 34, Hietalahti market hall, . Helsinki's first real ramen bar. Housemade noodles and popular tonkotsu broth. Big and fulfilling ramen soups from 11€.

Bar No 9, Uudenmaankatu 9, . Popular bar that also serves a variety of dishes with a twist of cross-kitchen style, priced from €4.90-15.90, most main courses under €10. Tends to be packed at lunch and dinner time.

Chilli, Keskuskatu 6 (*and other outlets around town*). Cheap kebab, shawarma, and falafel. Large portions, though be warned that this isn't your traditional Middle Eastern fare. Pitas come with something akin to spaghetti sauce inside. Filling choice, especially on a budget.

Event Arena Bank, Unioninkatu 20. Free flow lunch restaurant that offers a spacious and luminous environment to spend the lunch hour. The daily Lunch Club menu consists of four different choices all for

9,20€. There is choice of Scandinavian style home-cooking, Merranean or Asian delicacies, salad bar and soup of the day or vegetarian meal.

<u>Fredan Murkina</u>, Fredrikinkatu 16, Very simple and inexpensive lunch place, no gourmet-stuff going on here, but the sort of food Finns eat at home made fresh on site. Run by a friendly husband and wife team, this kiosk/restaurant melange a stone's throw away from five corners serves one of the cheapest healthy warm lunches you can eat in central Helsinki. Take away also possible if the few tables are full. At the time of writing (A day in Sep-'15) a soup cost 4.50 while lunch of the day was 5.70 or 7 depending on portion size.

<u>Golden Rax</u>, Aleksanterinkatu 11, Turunlinnantie 6 (Itäkeskus), . Cheap and greasy, all-you-can-eat pizza buffet. Includes soggy pasta, wilted salad, and drinks. €9.95 per person, €2.95 extra if you want ice-cream.

<u>Happiness Thai Buffet</u>, Helsingin yliopisto Metro station. Open M-F 11AM-8PM, Sa Su noon-7PM.

Decent Thai food with vegetarian options in an all-you-can-eat buffet, single dishes also available. Do yourself a favor though, and pass on the coffee. Buffet €9.50 (€10 with sushi), single servings ~€9.

<u>Kahvila Suomi</u>, Pursimiehenkatu 12, tel. *+358 9* 657422. Huge portions of tasty no-nonsense Finnish food like meatballs and mashed potatoes, which explains the dock workers that crowd here at lunchtime. The Japanese tourists, on the other hand, come because the cult hit movie *Kamome Shokudo* was filmed here! Most mains under €10, priced sandwiches available. Open M-F till 9 pm.

<u>La Famiglia</u>, Keskuskatu 3, tel. *+358 9* 85685680, . 11AM-midnight daily. Unpretentious Italian food even for under €10, although the most of the items on the menu should be listed under the Mid-price section. The weekday lunch buffet of soup, salad and two kinds of pasta (€7-10) is still a particularly good value.

Pasta La Vista, Mikonkatu 8 (*Ateneum*), . Pick a pasta, a filling and a sauce, for €7.70-8.70. Menu changes often, vegetarian options also available.

Pelmenit, Kustaankatu 7 (*Close to Sörnäinen metro station*), +358 41 783 9069, . M-Th 11:00-17:00, F-Su: 10:00-22:00. Serves *pelmeny*(Russian dumplings), *blini* (Russian crepes), soups and salads. The menu depends on the mood of the Russian owner. Around €10 for a dish..

Sky Express, Annankatu 31. A pizza spot very close to the city center. It's a relatively small place, but the service is very fast and the place is open late at night. Opens around 11AM, and closes at 11PM (10PM on Sundays). Try the *Päivän jättipizza* ("Daily giant pizza"), which is a large, thin pizza with a varying selection of fillings plus a 0.4 liter soft drink for €12,

Unicafe Ylioppilasaukio, Mannerheimintie 3 B, . Open M-F 11AM-7PM, Sa 11AM-5PM. The biggest and most centrally located student restaurant and cafeteria is only a two-minute walk away from the main railway station. The lunch price is only €6.10 including drink, bread and the salad buffet, and €2.50 if you happen to own a Finnish student card.

<u>Pompier</u>, Albertinkatu 29, . M-F 11AM-3PM. Run by the Volunteer Fire Brigade, this restaurant serves a daily changing buffet of hearty Finnish fare in a cafeteria straight from the 1950s, complete with grim portraits of moustached Hosemasters staring down at you. Pea soup and pancakes on Thursday are particularly popular. €10,00 per head.

<u>Singapore Hot Wok</u>, Kamppi Shopping Centre, E floor, Urho Kekkosen katu 5 B. Select from a few tasty plates of Wok. €9.50 per head.

Mid-range
Finnish
Cafe Balzac, Iso Roobertinkatu 3-5, , A nice place to pop in if you are walking through the so called "design district" area. Well hidden on an inner yard this french-style cafe/pub/restaurant one man show is a really nice find.

Kaarna, Mannerheimintie 20, +358 10 76 64550. Scandinavian-style restaurant with a location as central as it can get. Pop in from the main street for a glass of bubbly at the bar downstairs or settle in at the second floor for some Scandinavian-style tapas, or *snapas*, or other Nordic delicacies. Open Mon-Thu 11-23, Fri-Sat 11-24, Sun 12-21. Mains from 16 € to 30 €.

Kuu, Töölönkatu 27, . Restaurant Kuu has been offering Finnish specialities in the bohemian Töölö-district since 1966. Completely renovated a couple of years ago, the refreshed restaurant is more popular then ever before. A really good and decently priced wine-list, from the dishes the smoked salmon soup (9,50e/14,40e) is a real classic.

Cella, Fleminginkatu 15, . Established 1969, this is one of the oldest restaurants in the Kallio disctrict, serving classic Finnish food with lots of grease and salt. For a "real" restaurant (not fast food) in Helsinki it's reasonably priced, around € 10-20 for main dishes. The chef himself often serves the food, complete with a sexist joke or an insult, and may even force feed you the leftovers if you don't finish your meal! Also serves as a pub with a decent selection of beers, ciders and single malts.

<u>FishMarket</u>, Pohjoisesplanadi 17, *+358 9 6128 5250*

Finnish seafood restaurant and only seafood bar in Helsinki. Situated in the city center at the corner of the Kauppatori market place. Open Mon-Thu 18.00–23.00, Fri-Sat 17.00–23.30.

<u>Juuri</u>, Korkeavuorenkatu 27, *+358 9* 635 732, . Tiny restaurant known for its special Finnish entrées called *sapakset* (a play on *tapas*), with roots in Finnish food tradition. Try the cabbage roll with crayfish or the egg cheese with marjoram. All *sapakset* €4.3, main dishes €24. Lunch sets €7.5-10. Open M-F 11AM-2PM (lunch) & 4PM–10PM (à la carte), Sa noon-10PM, Su 4PM-10PM.

<u>Kuu Kuu</u>, Museokatu 17, . A cosy modern bar/restaurant. Populated by local actors and artists, this newly renovated place offers easygoing, simple Finnish food. Serves food until midnight on weekdays (that is very late in Finland) and is also a nice place for drinks. Still relatively free from tourists so don't expect hearing anything else but finnish and swedish here (staff is still multilingual). Mo - Fr 11-01, Sa 12-01, Su 12-22.

<u>Kappeli</u>, Eteläesplanadi 1, . Traditional Finnish dishes - reindeer, fish, etc. Some of the prices are on the high end of mid-range, but you should get polite service and well-prepared food with a lovely presentation. Cozy, relaxed, relatively quiet atmosphere (although the restaurant is apparently well-known and therefore might be more crowded during late evenings & tourist season). The roasted lamb with garlic potatoes is a good choice, as is their take on Finnish-style blueberry pie. They also offer a cheaper self-service cafe on the left side of the restaurant,

along with a bar (opened in 1867) in the middle of the building. Main lunch dishes €14-18, main dinner dishes about €15-36.

Konstan Möljä, Hietalahdenkatu 14, *+358 9* 694 7504, . Traditional Finnish food. Lunch buffet €7.90, main dishes €15+, dinner buffet €18. Very nice if you want to try all kinds of Finnish meals!

Kosmos, Kalevankatu 3, *+358 9* 647 255, . A Helsinki institution dating to 1924, proudly serving "Helsinkian" food a melange of Russian, French and Swedish influences. Try one of the three classics: Vorschmack with duchess potatoes, the Sylvester Sandwich *au gratin* and Baltic herrings with mashed potatoes. Mains €15-25. Trams: 2, 3, 4, 6, 7A/7B 10

Kynsilaukka (Garlic), Fredrikinkatu 22, *+358 9* 651939, . Good Finnish-influenced food from people truly dedicated to garlic. From the wonderfully intense garlic butter served with the bread to the sometimes subtle, sometimes *not* so subtle overtones in most of the dishes, this place is a delight for the garlic lover. Portion sizes are large, so if you're saving room for dessert (and you should), either skip the starters or else order the smaller size of both starter and main dish. The cinnamon pie dessert is particularly recommended. Main dishes €12-28. Trams: 3B/T. Open M-F 11AM-11PM, Sa Su 1PM-11PM.

Manala, Dagmarinkatu 2, *+358 9* 5807 7707, . The name may mean "Hell" and their motto "For devilish hunger and hellish thirst", but it's actually an understated white-linen-cloth restaurant serving traditional Finnish food and wood-fired pizzas. Open 11AM-4AM (Sa Su 2PM-4AM), lunch menus M-F 11AM-2PM. Main dishes €10-18. Trams: 4, 7A/B, 10.

Messenius, Messeniuksenkatu 7, tel. *+358 9* 2414950, . This fine neighbourhood place outside the city centre is famed for the "catch of the day", often caught by the fishing enthusiast owners themselves. Also fairly good steaks for the carnivores amongst us.

Perho, Mechelininkatu 7, *+358 9* 508 786 49, . Run by a cooking school, the cooks and waiters are all enthusiastic students, so the quality of food and service are good. Serves traditional Finnish and Russian food, set menus €20 to €30 including wine. Open M-Sa 11AM-11PM, Sun noon-5PM.

Ravintola N:o 11 (Restaurant Nr. 11), Pihlajatie 34, *+358 9* 477 2863, . This classic neighbourhood eatery in the Meilahti district, long known as *Kuusihokki*, recently reverted to its original 1946 name by its new owners who also improved the kitchen. The menu consists of basic but superbly executed classics such as salmon soup. The fantastic original 40s interior is also worth seeing.

Sea Horse, Kapteeninkatu 11, *+358 9* 628 169, . Established in 1933 as a basic eatery, this joint has slowly become a local legend affectionately known as *Sikala* ("Pigsty"), and both the decor and the menu are still preserved from the 1950s. A long-time Wallpaper Magazine favourite. Try the famous herring dishes or the onion steak. Meals between €10-30.

Sävel, Hämeentie 2 & Runeberginkatu 40, Finbistro with two locations, one in Hakaniemi (near the metro station) and one in Töölö (tram 2). Nice retro athmosphere and relatively late opening hours. Good place for huge and tasty hamburgers. Lunch buffet availabe as well. *+358 774 1082 +358 447555959*

Tori, Punavuorenkatu 2, small and cozy urban restaurant with laid-back style, offering European and Merranean food. Frequented mostly by young people and seems to be popular with Asian tourists. Excellent place to try authentic Finnish meatballs. No alcohol served. *+358 68743790*

Weeruska, Porvoonkatu 18, *+358* (0)20 7424 270, . Serves simple, but tasty, home-made style food. The clientele at lunch is primarily blue-collar workers and the portions are sized accordingly. Meals between €8-17.

Zetor, Kaivopiha, Mannerheimintie 3-5, +358 10 76 64450 , . Tourist restaurant with lots of character and great quality Finnish food. Plenty of old tractors and Finnish memorabilia. Main meals between €10-20.

International
Central Helsinki is dominated by restaurants dedicated to international cuisine, and these are particularly useful for vegetarian visitors, Finnish food being largely meat-based. A particular touch is provided by a bunch of "Nepalese" restaurants, which also serve generic north Indian food, but almost any of which you are guaranteed to leave happy and full. Localized Chinese and Italian cuisines are also well represented.

China Tiger, Korkeavuorenkatu 47, +358 9 949 5098 (), . Mon-Fri 11:00-23:00, Sat-Sun 12:00-23:00. Chinese food, adapted to local tastes. Lunch €9.2, mains from €12.8.

Brasserie Kämp, Pohjoisesplanadi 29, +358 9 5840 9530 (), . M-W 11:30AM–midnight, Th-F 11:30AM–1PM, Sa noon–1PM, Su noon–midnight. </eat .

Belge, Kluuvikatu 5 (*Kauppakeskus Kluuvi*), *+358 9 6229620*, . A reasonable selection of Belgian beers, a nice range of bistro fare, and a good location for people watching. The dining room upstairs is non-smoking. Main dishes €12–17.

Benjam's Bistro, Dagmarinkatu 5, tel: *+358 9 492 322*. You want home made Italian cooking in Helsinki? Here it is. Benjam's is run by an Italian family. Atmosphere is cozy, but some of the food comes directly from the supermarket, tortellini and many desserts, for example. The place is quite small and can easily get crowded; their sister place Zio Pepe at Lapinlahdenkatu 25 usually has more room. Main dishes €10–15.

Mountain, Nordenskiöldinkatu 8, tel: *+358 9 454 0501* . A nice Nepalese restaurant in Taka-Töölö. Main dishes 10-20 €. Lunch 9 € at 12-15.

Pikku-Nepal, Annankatu 29, *+358 9 6931778*. A good "Nepalese" restaurant. Main dishes €13–25. Good vegetarian options.

Everest, Luotsikatu 12 A, *+358 9* 6942563. A well-known "Nepalese" restaurant. Main dishes €10-20.

Gastone, Korkeavuorenkatu 45, *+358 9* 666116. . Nice restaurant with an Italian flavor. Reservations suggested, particularly on the weekend.

Mai Thai, Annankatu 31-33, *+358 9* 685 6850, . One of the better known Thai restaurants in Helsinki! Make sure to reserve a table in advance, and heed the chilli ratings when ordering.

Mandarin Court, Lönnrotinkatu 2, *+358 9* 278 2700. Finland's first attempt at an authentic Chinese restaurant, seems to get watered down more and more every year but still has a nice selection of dim sum. Main dishes €11–15.

Meze Point, Mikonkatu 8, *+358 9* 6222 625. Merranean meze plates, several vegetarian dishes. Excellent vegetarian moussaka. Main dishes €15-20.

Mt. Everest, Lapinlahdenkatu 17, +358 *9* 6831 5450, . Good Nepalese food. Main dishes €10-20.

New Bamboo Center, Annankatu 29, *+358 9* 6943117. Well-known downtown Malaysian-Chinese restaurant. Cheap lunch/dinner. Vegan-friendly with several vegan dishes. If you like elbow room you might want to pass on this restaurant, since the seating is somewhere between "intimate" and "cramped". The food is good, though.

Parilla Steak House Jätkäsaari, Tyynenmerenkatu 9, *+358 44* 480 9521. Steak restaurant located next to Helsinki West Harbour and Verkkokauppa.com electronics store. Eat while watching ferries arriving to the harbour. 70 seats. Ala carte and lunch buffet.

Sawat Dee, Alppikatu 5, *+358 9* 773 2745. Serves tasty Thai food in a milieu resembling backwoods gas station bar. Main dishes €10-12, lunch set €7.5.

Suola, Annankatu 6, +358 9 2709 0970 (), . Mon-Tue 11:00-00:00, Wed-Thu 11:00 - 02:00 (04) Fri 11:00 - 04:00 Sat 14:00-04:00 Sun 16:00-22:00. Located in the busy Punavuori district this nicely decorated place classifies itself as a modern bistro. Vibrant in the evenings as well, great choice for cocktails. Kitchen open until 22:00 daily. Lunch 8-15€, mains from 16€.

Empire Plaza, Urho Kekkosen katu 1, Kamppi Shopping Centre. Tasty Chinese food. Main dishes €7-20, lunch buffet €8.5.

Colorado Bar & Grill, Simonkatu 9. Tex-Mex. Main dishes €10-25.

Cantina West, Kasarmikatu 23. Tex-Mex. Pork Baby Ribs(€18). Main dishes €10-25.

Tamarin, Iso Roobertinkatu 18, Fredrikinkatu 49, Eteläesplanadi 4. Tasty Thai food. Main dishes around €14, lunch buffet €8.5.

Vegetarian
Just Vege, Vaasankatu 15, *+358 9* 759 3958 , . Vegetarian and vegan street food in Kallio. Try the goat cheese burger or the falafel pita with feta and marinated eggplant. Open daily until 10PM (Mon-Thu) / 2AM (Fri-Sun).

Silvoplee, Toinen linja 3, *+358 9* 726 0900, . Vegetarian restaurant specializing in living and raw foods but also serves warm dishes. Buffet, pay per weight. Closed on Sun.

Veganissimo, Kulmavuorenkatu 2, . Vegan lunch cafe. *Closed until further notice as of January 2015*

Zucchini, Fabianinkatu 4. Cozy vegetarian lunch restaurant with a daily changing soup and main dish (around €10). Open M-F 11AM-4PM (lunch served the whole time).

Splurge
Two classes of fine dining stand out in Helsinki: fresh seafood and Russian. During the dark days of the Soviet Union, it was sometimes said that the best Russian restaurants in the world were across the border in Helsinki. For something authentically Finnish and uniquely Helsinki, try *Vorschmack*, an unusual but surprisingly tasty mix of minced lamb and herring, served with chopped pickles and sour cream (*smetana*).

Finnish

<u>Carelia</u>, Mannerheimintie 56, tel. *+358 9* 27090976 Finnish-French with a strong fish and seafood emphasis. Oysters and other seafood in winter, local fish in the summer season. Located in the premises of an old pharmacy with some of the pharmacy interior still intact. One of the best (if not *the* best) wine cellars in town: there are 37 different champagnes alone on the wine list.

<u>Chef & Sommelier</u>. Huvilakatu 28, tel. *+358 400 959440*, . A small restaurant representing Nordic style cuisine and emphasizing on organic and local ingredients. Dishes are often served by the chefs themselves and you can really see the love and devotion they put into everything they serve. Voted 8th of "Top 50 Restaurants in Finland" in 2012. Bib Gourmand recognition as of 2011. Vegetarian and vegan menus also available. Open Tuesday to Saturday. Reservations essential.

<u>Demo</u>. Uudenmaankatu 9-11, tel. *+358 9 2289 0480*, . An unusual high-class restaurant geared towards the young and trendy, Demo's decor is minimalistic, but the food is of excellent caliber. There are no menus, only set courses pre-chosen based on what is fresh and available for the evening. Easily deserving of its Michelin star. Reservations essential.

<u>Olo</u>, Kasarmikatu 44, tel. *+358 9* 665 565, Combines North European ingredients into a modern Scandinavian cuisine while using seasons best ingredients available. Chosen as the best restaurant in Finland in 2012 by Viisi Tähteä magazine. One Michelin star.

<u>Rivoli</u>, Albertinkatu 38, tel. *+358 9* 643455. Traditional fine dining restaurant quite close to the SAS Royal and Scandic Simonkentta hotels. Specialities include oysters, shellfish and mussels in season (this was the first place in Finland to import them) and zander in an onion and cream sauce (traditional style).

International

<u>Farang</u>, Ainonkatu 3, +358 9 4544 212 (), . Tu-Sa 5PM-midnight. Farang serves interpretations of South-East Asias dishes in a modern decor. Try one of the Tasting Menus if you can't decide what to have. Mains €24–28, tasting menus €62–66.

<u>Farouge</u>, Yrjönkatu 6, *+358 9* 6123455. Probably the only real Lebanese restaurant in Finland. Friendly service and excellent food. Main dishes €14–38. Lunch M–Sa 11AM–3PM Closed Sun.

<u>Kabuki</u>, Lapinlahdenkatu 12, *+358 9* 694 9446, . Helsinki's best-known Japanese restaurant. Alas, while the food is decent, it's not quite the real thing. Reservations recommended for dinner. Closed Sat.

<u>Tokyo55</u>, Runeberginkatu 55, +358 10 841 1111, . Tu–F 4PM–midnight, Sa 2PM–midnight. The speciality here is sushi, served up by Japanese chefs, but there are also Finnish-styled options like *maki* rolls with smoked salmon and dill. Good selection of sake and Japanese beers. €30.

Yume, Kluuvikatu 2, +358 9 5761 1718 (), . Tue-Sat 17-24. Modern Asian cuisine. Part of the famous Luxury Collection Hotel Kämp . Mains 23–29 €, tasting menus 46–62 €.

Drinking

Helsinki has plenty of hip places for a drink. The main nightlife districts, all in the city center within crawling distance of each other, are around Iso-Roobertinkatu, the Central Railway Station and Kamppi. Helsinki's busy gay nightlife is centered mostly around Iso-Roobertinkatu and Eerikinkatuand surrounding streets.

Going out is not cheap, and complaining about the prices is a popular Finnish pastime, but compared to (say) London or New York City the prices aren't that bad. If you are on a budget and intent on getting plastered, follow the Finns and drink up a good "base" at home or hotel before going out on town. Alternatively, you can start the night outside the city centre area and head to the district of Kallio where bar prices are significantly lower. Popular places include Heinähattu, Roskapankki, Iltakoulu, Bar Molotow and Lepakkomies but there are lots more to choose from, just walk along Helsinginkatu or Vaasankatu. You can reach Kallio from the center by walking, by tram (lines 1, 3B, 6 or 7B) or by metro (get off at Hakaniemi and walk uphill, or Sörnäinen, and head west). Most bars close their doors between 2AM and 5AM, in city centre there are many that are open until 5AM. Kallio is usually considered as 'party starting district' but it's also common for locals to spend the whole night in Kallio, changing bar every now and then. The Kallio area is generally a bit rougher than the rest of the city and is as close as Helsinki gets to a red light district. However, it is a lot more tame than most 'such parts of town' in Europe. You will be fine there at any hour as long as you look out not to get in between a fight of two drunkards about who the remaining vodka belongs to.

Note that, while entry to bars and clubs is often (but not always) free, in club-type places and proper restaurants you must use and pay for the coat check(narikka), usually around €2, if you're wearing anything more than a T-shirt. In some places you must pay even if you don't leave anything at the cloakroom. The bouncer will be very strict with this as the much of the narikka-money goes into his pocket. If a ticket price is advertised, it usually does not cover the coat check.

The drinking age is 18, and this is rather strictly enforced, so bring along ID. Underaged drinking is still a huge problem, and many bars and clubs apply house limits of 20-24 years, but these are enforced less strictly and a patron of younger age will some times be let in if one fits the clientele, especially women.

Information on clubs and live performances can be found in free, Finnish-language tabloids such as City , which can be picked up at many bars, cafes and shops.

Cafes

Finland is the largest coffee consuming nation per capita and coffee breaks are written into law. However, in Finland most coffee is filter-brewed from a light, more caffeinated, roast that is quite different to what the rest of the world drinks. Finns often enjoy a bun (*pulla*) or cinnamon bun (*korvapuusti*) with their coffee.

In Finland commonly espressos and lattes are called "special coffees" and a large number of establishments that make such coffees have popped up all over town ever since the nineties when they arrived. One which will give any Italian cafeteria a go for their money is La Torrefazione next to Stockmann. In the more common cafeterias the normal light brew coffee is sold by self service at the counter even at some more expensive cafeterias (there is only a handful of cafeterias serving to the table in Helsinki - this shows how commonplace coffee drinking is considered).

<u>Cafe DaJa</u>, Mariankatu 13 B (*in the beautiful Kruununhaka district, 5 minutes from the Dom*). One of

the best Cafes in Helsinki with a german Kaffee Kultur. Very relaxed, excellent service, a awesome breakfast buffet every day and the best Flammkuchen in Town.

Ateljee Baari, Hotel Torni (*14th floor*), Kalevankatu 5. Despite the name it's more like a cafe, located on top of Hotel Torni, Finland's first high-rise. Excellent views over Helsinki's downtown. You even have a view from the (famous) toilets. Highly recommended. Find the elevator close to the lobby to get there, but be prepared for expensive drinks. If you're on a tight budget, you can just enjoy the view on the elevator level.

Café & Eepos, Runeberginkatu 29. A hidden gem near Temppeliaukion kirkko. Delicious pastries, pies and buns - and it's full of books you can read. There are even glasses available for those with poor eyesight.

Café Ekberg, Bulevardi 9, (09) 6811 860, . One of the classic Helsinki cafés.

Cafe Engel, Aleksanterinkatu 26 (*opposite the Lutheran cathedral*). Where the locals go for tea and snacks. Very relaxed, lovely courtyard out the back with films projected late into summer evenings.

Café Kafka, Pohjoisesplanadi 2 (Swedish *Theatre*). A lovely building with a relaxed atmosphere. Here you can find one of the best espressos in town. *Closed as of Summer 2010 due to renovations*

Cafe Succès, Korkeavuorenkatu 2, tel. *+358 9* 633414. This traditional cafe serves excellent delicacies. Famous for their enormous cinnamon rolls (*korvapuusti*), also available in Cafe Esplanad .

Café Tin Tin Tango, Töölöntorinkatu 7 (*tram 2, 8*), +358-9-27090972, . M-F 7AM-midnight, Sa-Su 9AM-2AM. A uniquely Helsinki combination of cafe, restaurant, bar, laundromat and sauna, Tin Tin Tango serves up all-day breakfast, soups, salads and sandwiches, but stays open late with wine and occasional live music. Laundry/dryer €4/2. Sauna is no longer in use.

Espresso Edge, Liisankatu 29, . A cozy bohemian café with a South American vibe, popular among the artsy types of the Kruununhaka neighbourhood, and Faculty of Social Science students from across the street.

Gran Delicato, Kalevankatu 34, tel. +358 9 694 0403. A very cosy cafe serving Merranean salads and paninis, and a variety of coffees. The Greek owner is a showman, usually around to amuse customers. Coffees 2-4€, salads 7-9€, pastas and soups 7-9€. Open weekdays 8.00-22.00, Saturdays 10.00-18.00, Sundays closed.

Kaffecentralen, Museokatu 9. This little shop concentrates on selling espresso paraphernalia, and also serves excellent capuccino.

Kahvila Sävy, Kinaporinkatu 1, . Small, retro style café with excellent coffee from a Finnish roastery. There are only a few seats in the former barbershop, next to the Sörnäinen metro. Also peculiar percolators for sale.

Kakkugalleria, Erottaja 7, . French-type cafe in the Design Forum. Try the lovely Sacher cake. Take away is cheaper.

Kipsari, Hämeentie 135 E, . Student cafe at the University of Art and Industrial Design in Arabia. Relaxed atmosphere with live music and DJs at times. Not open during summer when the school's out.

Sinisen huvilan kahvila, Linnunlauluntie 11 (*Töölönlahti, up the hill*). 10AM-10PM during summertime. The "Cafe of the Blue Villa" is an outdoors café with fantastic views over the Töölönlahti bay. Small coffee €1.5.

Käpylän lippakioski* A small kiosk built for the 1952 Helsinki olympics now has a cafe. It's a very relaxed hippie place with flexible prices. There are also lots of events in the park directly behind it. Easily accessible in the green Käpylä district a stone throw from the last stop of tram 1.

Bars and pubs
A21 Cocktail Lounge, Annankatu 21, . A high-priced but incredibly high quality cocktail bar situated in the city center, a few hundred meters from Stockmann's. Generally serves classic cocktail drinks with a twist, but also features several cocktails with a distinctly Finnish vibe (featuring garnishes such as birch leaves and fresh cloudberry) and innovative house specialities. According to worldsbestbars.com, this unlikely find is one of the world's best bars , winning the title of the best bar in the world in 2009 and 2010. Drinks €7-25, try the *Birch Cooler*, *Blinker* or *XXX*.

Ahjo, Bulevardi 2 (*Klaus K*), tel. +358-20-7704711. Named after the forge where the mythical Sampo of the Kalevala was made, this is a slick modern bar-lounge with two sides to it: a pure white space as you enter, with a bar counter and sofas, and a darker back room with nooks and crannies for a quieter chat. Drinks €6-8, try the *Ahjotonic*. Closed Sundays.

Aussie Bar, Salomonkatu 5, right next to the station. The name says it. Place to go get some drinks with some international fun. Live music every Wednesday and the weekends are always crazy in Kangaroo Land... Open Mon - Tue, Sun: 14:00 - 2:00 and Wed - Sat: 12:00 - 3:00.

Baarikärpänen. Located in Mikonkatu, right next to the Main Railway Station. Offers R & B and Top 40 hits in a nice lounge-type bar with big comfortable sofas and a dance floor. Reasonably cheap.

Bar Molotow, Vaasankatu 29, Small and always cozy indie/alternative/electro/goth rock bar. Nice summer terrace. Located in Kallio/harju district.

Baker's, Mannerheimintie 12, . A great place to start up your party. From Tues to Sat they have a sparkling wine happy hour from 5PM: for 100 minutes, a glass of *cava* costs 100 cents (that's one euro). The service might be somewhat rough. Also lots of young people there on weekends. Has a bar, nightclub, pub and serves also food.

Black Door, Iso Roobertinkatu 1, . English pub. Weekdays are relaxed, weekends have live DJs and a full bar. A place to go for quality beers, ales, ciders and whisky.

Corona Bar & Billiards, Eerikinkatu 11, (+358-9) 751 75611, . A bar and billiard hall owned by the film director brothers Aki and Mika Kaurismäki, echoing the melancholic mood of their films. Also check out the affiliated Kafe Moskva bar next door for authentic Soviet style experience, complete with Russian music played on dusty vinyls and Russian vodka and champagne. Downstairs is Dubrovnik , a small club-cum-movie theater that can be rented for private events and host occasionally live gigs or clubs..

Juttutupa, Säästöpankinranta 5, . In a nice old granite house called Graniittilinna you'll find (probably) Helsinki's oldest still operational pub, Juttutupa.

Juttutupa is housed in the "workers house" and has historically been the Bar of the policial left. In fact, while Lenin was hiding out in Finland planning the upcoming Russian revolution he was known to frequent Juttutupa, where the table he used to sit at is kept in his memory (the one in the back with a good view of the entrance). On Wednesdays there are often free Jazz concerts. Juttutupa also serves food from the neighboring restaurant's kitchen.

Erottaja Bar, Erottajankatu 15-17, tel. *+358 9* 611 196. A small, consciously crude bar, that formerly was known as one of the primary hipster hangouts in central Helsinki. The bar is now all but deserted by the trendy crowd, and the music turned into the usual fare of hit-list pop, but on the upside the service is friendly and there is ample sitting room at the tables.

Korjaamo, Töölönkatu 51, tel. *+358 9* 4540 117, . One of the best places to hang out at summer, nice terrace, two floor laid back bar with life DJ's in the evening and cafe in the building of the Korjaamo Cultural Factory.

Free access to Apple computers with Internet, Wi Fi. Café open daily 11AM–5PM, bar M Tu 4PM–11AM, W Th 4PM-1AM, F Sa 4PM–3AM, Sundays closed.

Molly Malone's, Kaisaniemenkatu 1, . An Irish pub/nightclub near the Central Railway Station. Popular among Finns and tourists alike. Live music every night.

Loose, Annankatu 21, . A very street-credible rock bar, it is highly popular among Finnish rock musicians.

Oluthuone Kaisla, Vilhonkatu 4, +358 10 766 3850, . Sun-Thu 12-02, Fri-Sat 12-03. Probably the best beer selection in town or even entire Finland with around 30 taps and some 200 different bottled beers. All the British, Belgian and German favourites and some Finnish craft brews. Also one of the more expensive places to grab your pint.

On The Rocks, Mikonkatu 15 (*near Central Railway Station*), . Located next to Baarikärpänen and Texas, this is a rock-oriented bar with occasional live bands and stand up comedy acts. Minimum age 23.

Pikkulintu, Klaavuntie 11, . Multiple award-winner for "Best Finnish Beer Pub", 20+ taps from Finnish and Nordic microbreweries. Although bizarrely located in a sleepy suburb, it is easily accessible by metro: take the Vuosaari line and stop at Puotila. Take the "Puotilan metrotori" exit and walk forward a couple of blocks.

Siltanen, Hämeentie 13, . A popular hipster haunt from the owners of the next door *Kuudes Linja* club venue (see below). Part bar, part club and part café (with food served until 10PM) with a big terrace and weird décor. Open 11AM-2AM daily, with DJs and the occasional live gig in the evenings. Weekend DJ brunch noon-4PM, prepare to wait for a table though.

Sports Academy, Kaivokatu 8, . One of the best sports bars in Helsinki, and definitely the place for you if you are keen about football (soccer) or ice-hockey. A two-story building just opposite the railway station, filled to the rim with TV sets and several giant projectors. A variety of pub food also served - try the crayfish pasta or the ribs. There can be long queues before popular events - get in early!

<u>Toveri</u>, Castreninkatu 3, +358 9 753 3862, . You'll find various types of beer in this little bar. It's been here in various forms since 1937, and after its most recent transformation it is one of the prettiest bars in Kallio.

<u>Vanha ylioppilastalo</u> (usually just Vanha), Mannerheimintie 3, . A bar/café just opposite Stockmann, owned by University of Helsinki's filthy rich students' union. Not very special in the winter, but the rooftop patio in the summer is nice. In the evenings, the club attracts a slighly-over-18 audience.

<u>Siima Baari</u> Vaasankatu 25, An often rowdy bar in Kallio.

Nightclubs
In Helsinki, the most popular nightclubs have long queues starting to form around 11:30PM. Get in early to avoid standing, although it can be a nice way to

meet people. After around 1:00-2:00AM it might be impossible to get in anymore. You may try to just walk past the queue looking important, but a more efficient strategy is to discreetly tip the bouncer (€10-20). The larger group you are, the more difficult things get. Look smart!

Cuba, Erottajankatu 4, . A night club with a somewhat more "Latin" touch and softer tunes. Clientele mostly trendy young adults. Open until 4AM, often hosts student parties on weekday nights. No entrance fee.

DTM, Mannerheimintie 6 B, . Open M-Su 21:00-04:00. Formerly "Don't Tell Mama", DTM is the largest combination of gay cafe, bar, disco and nightclub in Scandinavia. Popular among many celebrities. Straights usually welcome, too, as long as they don't "take over" the place. Entrance €7-10 (Sat and special nights only).

Hercules Gay Night Club, Pohjoinen Rautatiekatu 21 B, . One of the busiest gay nightclubs in Scandinavia, targets a 30+ clientele, good for bare-faced cruising. Entrance free; coat check €2.50.

Vatican, Simonkatu 6. Vatican (former Jenny Woo) tries to profile itself as a nightclub for trendy young adults. You can lie on couches next to the crowded dance floor while sipping some bubbly.

Kaarle XII, Kasarmikatu 40, tel. *+358 9* 6129990, . A Helsinki institution better known as *Kalle*, this former church hasn't had a renovation in years and really needs one. It still continues to pack in a hard-partying thirtysomething crowd, especially on Thursdays. No less than six different bars (all small), playing top 40 tunes, rock and Finnish pop. The last of the bars has a dancefloor and gets particularly packed, with people dancing on the tables. Minimum age 24. Open Th-Sa 10PM-4AM.

Kaiku, Kaikukatu 4 *(in the inner court)*, . Techno and house by local DJs and international guests in an old factory building. Part of the same complex as Kuudes linja and Siltanen. Long queues on popular nights but it's usually worth it: Kaiku was listed among the 25 best clubs in Europe by Guardian . Tickets €8-15 (often free if you arrive early). Open F-Sa 10PM-4AM.

<u>Kuudes linja</u>, Hämeentie 13 *(entrance from the inner court at Kaikukatu 4)*, . A live music oriented nightclub for the somewhat artsy crowd next to Kaiku. Located a 10 min tram/bus ride away in the Kallio district, Kuudes linja usually offers more experimental/alternative music than the mainstream downtown clubs and also hosts electronic music parties. Arrive early to avoid queues on popular nights admittance is not guaranteed once the place gets full. The weatherproof terrace in the courtyard is open during the summer. Club open W, F, Sa 10PM-4AM, Th 9PM–4AM.

<u>Tavastia/Semifinal</u>, Urho Kekkosen katu 4-6, . One of the most prominent rock clubs in Scandinavia, a must see for fans of live rock of any kind. Semifinal has smaller indie/alternative bands for a young crowd. On special nights the two clubs are joined, but usually they host separate gigs. Tickets for all gigs can be bought in

advance from the Tiketti ticket sellers next door. The annual Tavastia new year party is an institution in itself, with fans flying from all over the world for the show.

<u>Teatteri</u>, Pohjoisesplanadi 2, . A complex featuring a deli, a restaurant, a bar and a night club, all of them trendy and popular among the well-dressed crowd. Check out the aptly named Clock Bar (*Kellobaari*) downstairs. Closed Sun.

<u>Ääniwalli</u>, Pälkäneentie 13, . A hip club focusing on electronic music. Underground vibes.

Sleep

Accommodation is generally quite expensive, but of a high standard. Hotels are usually *cheaper* on weekends, when business travelers are away. In a real pinch, it may actually be (far) cheaper to book a "last-minute" or "red-ticket" return cabin (from around Euro 20) on an overnight cruise to Tallinn, and spend the night (and part of the next day) on the boat, rather than sleep in the city.

Budget

There are quite a few budget hotels in Helsinki, the cheapest being youth hostels. Many student dormitories turn into youth hostels during the July-August school break, which happily coincides with peak season for tourists. The Finnish Youth Hostel Association can provide further information.

ThePark Helsinki by CheapSleep, Inarintie 8 (*Trams 1, 1A, 6, 7A, 7B, 8 numerous buses (inc. airport bus 615)*), . checkin: 14.00; checkout: 11.00. Helsinki's newest hostel, excellent transport connections, near social Kallio neighborhood, stylish vibe. Free sauna, onsite parking, fast free wifi, 24h reception. Opened in June 2016. Dorms from 19€ and private doubles from 79€ per room.

CheapSleep Helsinki, Sturenkatu 27 (*Trams 1, 1A, 7A, 7B, numerous buses (inc. airport bus 615)*), . checkin:

14.00; checkout: 11.00. Helsinki's second newest hostel, excellent transport connections, near social Kallio neighborhood, stylish vibe. Opened in May 2012. Kitchen used to be a little dirty, but overall tidy and nice place! Totally renovated during summer 2016, reopening 1st October 2016. Dorms from 16€ and private doubles from 69€ per room.

Eurohostel, Linnankatu 9 (*Tram 4 and 4T*), +358 9 6220470, . checkin: 14; checkout: 12. Helsinki's largest hostel, very close to the dock for the Viking Line ferry and the Uspenski Cathedral. Walking distance from the city centre. Dorms from €24.30, single rooms from €45,40, twin rooms from €54.20 and triple rooms from €72.90. Buffet breakfast €8.50. Morning sauna always included. 27.10.

Summer Hostel Karavaani, Karavaanikatu 4 (*Vuosaari metro line to Rastila*), +358 9 310 71441 (), . checkin: 16; checkout: 12. Family-friendly hostel open in June-July at Rastila Camping, just a quick metro ride away from the city centre. Rooms for 1 to 5 people, as well as beds in a dormitory. Bed linen included in the price. Dorm €21, private double room €62, family price (2 adults, 3 children) €77.

Hostel Erottajanpuisto, Uudenmaankatu 9, . A small, clean, and friendly hostel with a central location. €27€ for a dorm bed.

Hostel Suomenlinna, Suomenlinna C 9 (*ferry connection from Market Square*), . All year open hostel located at the Suomenlinna sea fortress. Great for a quick escape from the city. The ferry runs from 6am to 2am so you are not totally cut off.

Rastila Camping, Vuosaari (*M Rastila*), . The only camping site inside Helsinki borders. Seventeen minute metro ride from the Central Railway Station.

Summer Hostel Academica, Hietaniemenkatu 14 (*M Kamppi, Tram 2*), (, fax: +358 (9) 441 201), . Summer hostel in the heart of Helsinki. *Open June-August only*. Dorms from €25, hotel rooms from €50.

Traveller's Home, Lönnrotinkatu 16 D, . Central location, clean, and good amenities. Wi-fi €5/day. Fully-furnished flat from €85/night.

Kyronhostelli, Viides Linja 12, . A Hostel who provides low cost, yet high quality accommodation in the possibility of Helsinki. There are single, double and triple rooms. €20€ Par night.

Omenahotelli, . Omena hotels are self-service budget hotels with no front desk: book and pay on the Internet and let yourself in with a passcode. They have been established in most major Finnish cities and are used widely by Finns travelling in their own country. *Omena* means *apple* in Finnish. 3 hotels in Helsinki, all in the center: *Helsinki Eerikinkatu* (Eerikinkatu 24, near Kamppi), *Helsinki Yrjönkatu* (Yrjönkatu 30, close to Forum Shopping Centre), *Helsinki Lönnrotinkatu* (Lönnrotinkatu 13, close to Esplanadi). Prices start at €36/room (up to 4 people). Rooms include toilet, shower, free wi-fi, 26" LCD-television, small fridge, microwave, water kettle +

disposable cups, coffee, tea, hair dryer and dining table. Omena-breakfast 5,80 €/person. Business-package 16 €/night includes Internet connection, two volitional movie per day and breakfast. Parking 17,50 €/night.

Mid-range
Best Western Premier Hotel Katajanokka, Vyökatu 1, +358 9 686 450, . Housed in what was the *Nokka* prison until 2002, this classy hotel has retained the original exterior and the internal corridor, but the rooms themselves, built by combining two to three cells, retain no trace of their past. Walking distance to city center. From €99.

Best Western Hotel Carlton, Kaisaniemenkatu 3, +358 9 684 1320 (, fax: +358 9 660 112), . Best Western Hotel Carlton is a personal, 19 room hotel in the very center of Helsinki, only 100 metres from Helsinki Central Railway Station.

Best Western Hotel Haaga, Nuijamiestentie 10, +358 9 5807 877 (, fax: +358 9 5807 8386), . Best Western

Hotel Haaga is centrally located since it's only 15 minutes drive from Helsinki-Vantaa airport.

Cumulus Hakaniemi, Siltasaarenkatu 14 (*M Hakaniemi*), +358 (0)9 5466 0100, . A centrally located business hotel. From €83 for a double in the low season.

Cumulus Kaisaniemi, Kaisaniemenkatu 7 (*M Helsingin yliopisto*), . A centrally located but minimally equipped business hotel. From €83 for a double in the low season.

Cumulus Olympia, Läntinen Brahenkatu 2 (*Tram 3*), +358 (0)9 69151, . A business hotel near the city centre. From €83 for a double in the low season.

Hotel Finn, Kalevankatu 3B, +358 9 6844360 (, fax: +358 9 68443610), . checkin: 15.00; checkout: 12.00. A young, regenerating hotel right in the city center. Even though the rooms are small and fairly no-frills, the hotel is comfortable and cheap. There are 27 rooms, which can accommodate from one to four people per room. From 55€.

Helka, Pohjoinen Rautatiekatu 23 (*near M Kamppi*), . A dependable old standby within walking distance of the city center. Generally €~150.

Hotel GLO Airport, Helsinki-Vantaa Airport Terminal 2, +358 103 444 600 (, fax: + 358 103 444 601), . The only hotel located in the airport building itself, on the service floor of Terminal 2 and with direct indoor access from Terminal 1.Day Rooms are also made available for use, depending on the booking situation, between 9:00 - 19:00 .

Hotel GLO, Kluuvikatu 4, +358 9 5840 9540 (), . Hotel GLO is situated in the centre of Helsinki, between Alexanterinkatu and Pohjois Esplanadi.The hotel has a direct entrance to the shopping centre Kämp Galleria. The Palace Kämp Day Spa is located on the top floor of the hotel. Glo clearly lives of being the slightly cheaper alternative next door to Kämp, but is not quite able to match the quality of service of a true luxury hotel either.

Hotel Linna, Lönnrotinkatu 29, +358 10 3444 100 (), .

Hotel Room, Helsinginkatu 12, +358 40 833 6696 (), . Hotel Room is actually not a hotel, but a funkily furnished 30 sq.m. flat in the Kallio district. Around €100.

Scandic Continental Helsinki, Mannerheimintie 46, +358 (0)9 4737 1 (, fax: +358 (0)9 4737 2211), . A large, modern hotel catering to families, leisure travelers, and business travelers. Over 500 rooms, sauna, exercise facilities, wireless Internet access, restaurant and bar. Excellent breakfast included with all rooms. Good location near Tram 4, 7, and 10 for convenient transport to city center (3 min by tram, or a 10 min walk). Finnair buses from the airport stop close to the hotel (about 2 blocks past on the way from the airport, and directly opposite the hotel on the way to the airport), providing convenient transport to/from airport. From €89.

Sokos Hotel Aleksanteri, Albertinkatu 34, +358 (0)20 1234 643 (, fax: +358 (0)20 1234 644), . Situated in the heart of the city in the trendy Punavuori neighbourhood, next to the historical Alexander Theatre. From €139.

StayAt Parliament, Museokatu 18, +358 9 2511 050 (, fax: +358 9 2511 0600), . A modern hotel in an old apartment building in the elegant residential district of Töölö, formerly *Accome Töölö*. Rooms are modern, spacious and have nice views to the park across the street and to the others architecturally beautiful buildings. A twin room goes for €77–128, a one bedroom room €96–176 and the biggest two bedroom apartment with a sauna and a balcony €110–184.

Splurge

Radisson Blu Royal, Runeberginkatu 2, +358 20 1234 701 (), . Located in the heart of the city centre, the architecturally distinct Radisson Blu Royal Hotel, Helsinki is an ideal home base for exploring this beautiful Finnish city. Stay in the area's lively business and entertainment district and enjoy the convenience of public transport as well as the Kamppi shopping centre, within walking distance of the hotel. On-site dining options include Michelin-rated Restaurant Grill it!, a self-serve coffee bar and a beverage bar. From €98.

Radisson Blu Plaza, Mikonkatu 23, +358 20 123 4700, . Classy hotel in a protected and carefully renovated, Kalevala-inspired 1917 building, located near the railway station within easy walking distance of Aleksanterinkatu. Excellent breakfast buffet. From €150.

Hotel Haven, Unioninkatu 17, 358 9 681930, . Hotel Haven, Finland's first member of the Small Luxury Hotels of the World, is designed to provide homely warmth, exclusive comfort and high-quality services for the discerning guest. From €169.

Crowne Plaza, Mannerheimintie 50, "+358, . Formerly the *Hotel Hesperia*. Rooms offer comfy beds, modern furniture and up-to-date electronics. The hotel also has a sparkling new gym with a pool. From €255.

Hilton Strand, John Stenbergin ranta 4, 358-9-39351 (fax: 358-9-3935-3255), . Located across the Pitkäsilta bridge, a 15-minute walk or short tram ride away from the main railway station.

Klaus K, Bulevardi 2, +358 20 7704700, . Helsinki's first boutique hotel, although they prefer the term "personal contemporary hotel". Rooms range from the small Passion & Mystical types to the aptly named Envy Plus. Central location, funky styling and reasonable prices make this a winner. From €115.

Hotel Kämp, Pohjoisesplanadi 29, +358 9 576111, . Opened 1887, this historic hotel claims to be the only true 5-star in Scandinavia, with doormen in top hats, yacht charters and prices to match: the eight-room Mannerheim Suite can be yours for only €3300 per night. Part of Starwood's Luxury Collection. Rooms from €120.

Stay safe

The crime rate in Helsinki was earlier generally low, although locals grumble that things have gotten worse since the EU removed restrictions on movement. Pickpockets target crowds and bicycles are prone to petty theft. Walking in the streets after dark is generally safe and the city center is indeed quite lively until the early hours of the morning. However, it's best to steer clear of obviously drunk people looking to pick a fight, the traditional trouble spots being the frustratingly long queues for late night snack food or taxis. Getting mugged for money in the streets of central Helsinki is almost unheard of, but you might not want to get into any unlicensed taxis even though the licensed ones are almost always way short of demand during pre-Christmas and summer seasons. A licensed taxi in Finland will always have a yellow box with its number on the roof.

The most crimes in city center concentrate around central railway station and Kamppi shopping center. The Kaisaniemi park behind the main Railway Station is possibly best avoided at night, and some parts of Kallio and Sörnäinen (northeast from the center, after the Pitkäsilta bridge) may be somewhat rougher than other parts of the downtown.

Finnish police never require a cash payment of fines which it gives. Never give money to a person who presents him/herself as a police officer. Ask the police officer to show his/her badge. Do not try to bribe a local authorities - it is illegal.

In winter, try to keep a steady footing: despite the use of vast quantities of gravel and salt, pavements can be quite slippery when the temperature hovers around zero and near-invisible black ice forms. Also especially in spring watch out for snow falling from the roofs of the buildings. After several injuries and even a few deaths, real property owners are now busy keeping the roofs clear of snow .

Every spring a few hundred Roma beggars from Romania and Bulgaria arrive in Helsinki to stay for the summer. This phenomenon exists in many European cities, but is particularly ample in Helsinki due to the fact that there are virtually no local beggars. For years these beggars were considered to be organized crime, but in the summer of 2013 the Finnish police stated that no such links exist . In very rare cases these beggars can become aggressive, but mostly they just beg on the sidewalk or collect bottles to get funds from reverse vending machines.

Helsinki's bedrock is close to the surface, so new building works invariably involve some dynamite to build foundations, and it's thus quite common to hear explosions around the center. Blasting is often preceded by a loud sequence of warning beeps, which speed up as they count down. There is no danger to anyone, as the builders are experts (and the solid granite bedrock is very, very strong), but now you know where that "BOOM!" came from.

If you are just passing through and choose Helsinki to apply for a Russian visa, be careful when choosing a travel agency: some may charge a lot extra for "express service" (although applying for one yourself at the consulate will take weeks).

Respect

As with many cities, when using escalators, people in Helsinki usually reserve the right-hand side for standing and the left-hand side for people walking up/down. If not sure, use the stairs.

It would also be wise to use common sense while boarding trains, trams or metros. Don't block people when the doors open. Let the people exiting the carrier get out first, then it's the entering people's turn. Likewise, when exiting trains, trams or metros, you have 'right of way', and should exit before others board.

Avoid walking on the cycle lane. Dedicated cycle paths are clearly marked, but sometimes run directly next to the sidewalk. Helsinki cyclists are subject to a comparatively hilly landscape and are unwilling to slow down and lose momentum. Usually, however, they are careful, signal clearly and use their bells, meaning that straying tourists most often are just sworn at, although you are free to swear back at them.

When waiting in lines, be patient and polite. Finns never jump queues so make sure you do not move and stand still in the line. If not sure, ask how to queue.

Finns usually don't address people who are doing things (in their opinion) wrong. They will just look at your foolish behavior, laugh silently to themselves and swear secretly behind you, but it is not unusual to hear nasty comments from strangers if you do things wrong, like ride a bicycle on a sidewalk.

Do not feed gulls or pigeons (especially in the city center). It is officially prohibited in many areas and even if not, locals will get irritated seeing someone throw anything edible to "flying rats", and again (you guessed it), they will swear at you.

Contact

Much of Helsinki is blanketed with wifi ("wlan") hotspots, and the City of Helsinki maintains a handy map . By comparison, Internet cafes with shared PCs are few and far between in Helsinki.

Library 10, Elielinaukio 2 G, tel. +358 9 3108 5000, . A public Internet and music library located in the main post office building at the western side of the central railway station. You can surf the Internet for free for 30 minutes on the library's computers , but you're going to have to queue. Also has wi-fi, but you need a library card to access the network.

Mbar, Mannerheimintie 22-24 (Lasipalatsi), tel. +358 9 612 4542, . A pleasant and popular living room-ish space in the heart of the city with local DJs playing drum & bass, house and chillout beats. Computers with Internet access (€5 per hour; €2 minimum charge), free wifi for laptop & cell phone owners. The terrace is a popular hipster hangout in the summer, situated in the former bus station area just next to the bar. Drinks €4-5.

Many internet/cyber cafes in Finland can be expensive. There are a large number of locations in Helsinki that offer free public wifi for those needing to connect to the office while outside of the country. Most cafes offer these services without requiring a person to be a paying customer. Some restaurants will do this as well, but may insist that you purchase something. There is a list of the free wifi locations compiled online .

Sightseeing in Helsinki

what to see. Complete travel guide

Sea had always played an important role in the foundation and development of the modern metropolis of Helsinki. This is the reason why the capital of Finland is often called the daughter of Baltic. Helsinki is the political and economic center of Finland. Helsinki residents have a reputation of tolerant and well-mannered people who appreciate art and nature. The city, which is home to a large number of parks and which is surrounded by forests, skerries and the sea, is distinguished by the Scandinavian maritime climate.

The architectural style of Helsinki is the mix of old and new buildings - czarist-era buildings adjoin modern palaces made of glass and metal. The city's landscape looks bright and vivid thanks to numerous cafes and markets. Clothing, jewelry or crafts featuring traditional Finnish design can be found everywhere in Helsinki.

Satama and Suomenlinna.

Helsinki port, Satama, is located right near the market. This is an important transit point for all arriving and departing passengers. From here tourists are welcome to make an excursion tour on a boat that will bring them around the Finnish capital. Tourists are also welcome to visit one of the nearby islands and the Helsinki Zoo. Suomenlinna is a place that certainly deserves special attention. This is a fortress built on one of the islands located in front of the port. The fortress appeared in the XVIII century, and its main aim was to protect Finland, which was ruled by the Swedes that time, from constantly attacking Russian troops.

Nowadays, Suomenlinna, is home to 850 residents. The fortress has also become a favorite place for country walks and relaxation for inhabitants of Helsinki. The largest sea fortress in whole Scandinavia can be reached by ferry. The ferry leaves from the port pier on Market Square. In addition to rocky coast, Suomenlinna, which is included in the list of world heritage sites by UNESCO, offers its visitors large green areas for picnics, old wooden houses with cafes or museums, a small hotel where visitors can stay for a night. This is also the place, where visitors will be able to see the only Finnish submarine of the World War II period. There is a church there that is also used as a beacon.

Church Temppeliaukion Kirkko.

The church in Temppeliaukion kirkko rock attracts visitors not only by its natural simplicity, but also by an excellent contrast to architecturally pretentious churches and oil paintings overloaded with all kinds of decorations and gold jewelry. Temppeliaukion kirkko emerged in the 60s of the previous century. The construction began with the fact that a large piece of rock was taken from the mountain. Because of this a hole appeared in the rock. The outer side of the rock was decorated with a round, rather low copper dome with built-in glass surfaces. This way the church is illuminated only by the light that penetrates the top of the dome and a little amount of candles that stand on the rocky ledges of the walls. A modest cross and several wooden benches are the only decorations of the interior of the church. Thanks to incredible acoustics, the church in the rock often becomes the venue for organ concerts. Copyright

Cathedral Tuomiokirkko.

Dazzlingly white on the inside and outside, Tuomiokirkko Cathedral is currently considered the most famous symbol of the capital of Finland. To get inside the cathedral, you will need to go up a long staircase. When the weather is good, the staircase is always full of people who come here to sunbathe or enjoy magnificent panoramic views of the port. If you have enough time, it is definitely better to follow your visit to Tuomiokirkko with an excursion to the Cathedral of the Assumption. The cathedral is located on the nearby Katajanokka peninsula. The cathedral is known as the most significant Orthodox Church in Finland. Gilded onion-shaped domes and walls made of red brick are very popular with travellers who are keen on photography. This Russian-Byzantine style of the church reminds of Russian reign in Finland, which lasted until 1917. Every year Katajanokka Peninsula is visited by approximately 500,000 tourists.

Olympic Stadium.

Olympic Stadium is located approximately two kilometers away from the historical center of Helsinki. This is the largest stadium in Finland, the symbol of which is a tall observation tower of 72.71 m. The tower's length is a bit strange, but it has a symbolic meaning. Its unusual length matches the length of the record spear throw of Matti Järvinen, a winner of the Olympic Games of 1932. The construction of the stadium was completed in 1938, but the summer Olympic Games of 1940, which were to be carried out there, were canceled due to the beginning of the Second World War. In 1952, Helsinki finally hosted the Olympics. During the games the Olympic Stadium was the main venue for competitions and it provided seats to more than 70,000 spectators. In late 90's the stadium was closed for a five year renovation, after which the capacity of the stadium was reduced to a maximum of 40 000 spectators. When the stadium does not host sports competitions or other activities, its observation tower, which offers a wonderful view of the capital of Finland, is open to visitors.

Seurasaari Island.

Seurasaari Island is located to the west of Helsinki. The island is famous for its open air museum that features Finnish buildings of XVII-XX centuries. Dressed in traditional costumes, the museum's guides will tell visitors about life of the Finns in the last century. Besides the museum, the island is famous for its picturesque landscapes, and everyone is welcome to admire this beauty for free. Many residents of Helsinki use this opportunity to come to Seurasaari in order to swim or have a picnic. The traditional favorite pastime of all visitors of the island is giving nuts to lovely squirrels. Every year the largest number of tourists comes to Seurasaari during the summer solstice, or the so-called white nights. The celebration dedicated to the summer solstice, which takes place between June 20 and 26, attracts both locals and tourists, who use loud music, hearty food, heavy drinking to scare off evil spirits.

Helsinki City Museum

The Helsinki City Museum is the world's only museum focusing on Helsinki. It is located in the oldest quarters of the city, at the corner of the Senate Square. It is a museum of everyday life, offering new perspectives to the history of the city, heart-warming details and many types of spaces and atmospheres. The permanent Helsinki Bites exhibition plunges into the history of Helsinki and collects shared memories of the past. In the Children's Town, generations meet and learn about the past by doing things together. The Time Machine offers time travel with the help of new technology. You'll also find a museum shop and café/wine bar El Fant in the building.

Burgher's House

Sneak in through the yellow gate and revel in the atmosphere of the 1860s in the oldest surviving wooden house in Helsinki.At the Burgher's House Museum, you can experience everyday life and living in a house of the bourgeois in the Kruununhaka district of the 1860s and 70s. Part of the Helsinki City Museum.

Villa Hakasalmi

The charming Villa Hakasalmi is located next to Finlandia Hall near Töölönlahti bay. This elegant building retains a tangible sense of the Empire style era and is one of the few of its kind remaining in Helsinki. The best-known resident of Villa Hakasalmi was Aurora Karamzin (1808-1902), who lived there until her death. Because of this, the building is also referred to as the Karamzin Villa. The villa is today a branch of the Helsinki City Museum with changing exhibitions. An idyllic cafe is located on the courtyard, serving coffee, snacks and a daily changing lunch.

Sederholm House Children's town at the Helsinki City Museum

By the Senate Square, in the oldest quarters of the city, lies the Sederholm House, completed in 1757. It is the oldest house in Helsinki, now part of the Helsinki City Museum and belongs to the youngest in the city. The Children's Town is a family favourite where generations meet and learn about the past by doing things together. Play in an 18th century shop, write on a blackboard or examine everyday artefacts in the 1970s grandma's house. At the Helsinki City Museum you'll also find a museum shop and café El Fant.

Worker Housing Museum

The atmospheric Worker Housing Museum and its little "stove rooms" tell a fascinating story about Finnish everyday life in the past. The museum is located in the oldest apartments built by the city for its own workers in Helsinki. The Worker Housing Museum is part of Helsinki City Museum. Museum is currently closed.

Tram Museum

Helsinki's oldest tram depot (1900) houses the Tram Museum which is part of Korjaamo culture centre in Töölö. The museum presents the history of trams in Helsinki from a passenger's point of view. At the Tram Museum, you can take a seat in an old tram that instantly transports you to the Helsinki of yesteryear. Branch of the Helsinki City Museum.

National Museum of Finland

Mon closed, Tue-Sun 11-18, Wed 11-20
The National Museum of Finland illustrates Finnish history from prehistoric times to the 19th century. The

museum's unique exhibits tell of life from a period of over 10 000 years. Temporary exhibitions on current themes and an interactive exhibition Vintti, where one can experience history by doing oneself. The National Museum building was designed by the Finnish architects Herman Gesellius, Armas Lindgren and Eliel Saarinen. With its granite façade and steatite decoration, the building is one of Finland's most significant national-romantic works of architecture. The museum was opened to the public in 1916. A café and museum shop are also located in the museum.

Seurasaari Island

Seurasaari is open all year. The open air museum is open in summer, please see Seurasaari Open-Air Museum.
The Seurasaari island provides a nice setting for outdoor recreation, sun worshippers and walkers. The tame ducks, swans and geese swarming around the bridge welcome everybody. Having crossed the white wooden bridge a visitor can't help running into the happy little squirrels of the island. At the Open-Air

Museum of Seurasaari the traditional Finnish way of life is displayed in the cottages, farmsteads and manors of the past four centuries that have been relocated from all around Finland. The Kalevalakehto Installation (2010) by students from American and Finnish schools of architecture and design is situated on the south bank of the island and is ment for relaxing and enjoying the silence. At Seurasaari you'll also find restaurant Seurasaari, Cafe Mieritz, kiosks and a beach (nude-, except for Wed & Sun). Barbecueing is also possible at the grill by the Festival Ground kiosk.

Tamminiemi

In October-March Sat-Sun 11-17, April-September Wed-Sun 11-17
Tamminiemi Villa is located in Meilahti adjacent to Seurasaari museum island on a beautiful park estate which used to be President Urho Kekkonen's official residence during his period in office between 1956 and 1981. In those days it was known as the centre of Finland's political and governmental life. Tamminiemi

is furnished the way it was in Kekkonen's time in the 1970's. Museum shop and Café Adjutant.

Suomenlinna Museum

During 1.10-31.12. Mon-Sun 10.30-16.30. During 2.1.-30.4. Mon-Sun 10.30-16.30. 2.5.-30.9. Mon-Sun 9.30-18. Closed: 1.1., 19.4., 24.-25.12
Suomenlinna Museum, located in the Suomenlinna Centre, showcases the eventful history of the sea fortress from the 18th century to the present day. It also depicts the restauration process of the fortress that is part of the history of three different countries - Sweden, Russia and Finland - and a UNESCO World Heritage Site since 1991. The wide-screen presentation "Suomenlinna Experience" offers the visitors an excursion to the fascinating history of Suomenlinna. The wide-screen presentation is shown in the museum every 30 minutes during the museum's opening hours. Last presentation an hour before closing time.

Family trip with kids

Family trip to Helsinki with children. Ideas on where to go with your child

Helsinki is an ideal city for family travel. Tourists with children can have fun time there in both winter and summer. There are many amusement parks in the city and each of them has its own strong points and peculiarities. Linnanmäki is considered one of the biggest entertainment complexes in the city. In order to try all the rides available there, one will need more than one day. Besides numerous slides and rides, merry-go-rounds, and playgrounds, this entertainment complex has a great aquarium, a visit to which will also please children. Quite an interesting fact there are special "winter aquariums" in the complex, and fish swim there under a thick layer of ice.

If large entertainment complexes are not your cup of tea, and you would prefer a calmer pastime instead, it's worth visiting the island-museum of Seurasaari. This place is very popular with locals who come to the island with children in order to walk in picturesque place and make a picnic. Seurasaari is also famous because of Open-Air Museum, a visit to which will be also very interesting for children. The museum is dedicated to the culture of Finland, and new items regularly appear there, so even travelers who have already visited the museum in the past will find it amusing to visit it again. A large part of the island is covered with woods that have become home for many cute squirrels that are absolutely not afraid of people.

The abundance of playgrounds for children is one of the advantages of Helsinki. It's simple to find quality playgrounds in literally every district and close to all popular streets. Tourists who visit these playgrounds with kids should remember about a very important and useful service. It is called "Family House" a special house where visitors can change clothes of their children or heat their food. These charming houses allow mothers with babies enjoy comfortable open air walking or playing. Copyright

There are many interesting museums in Helsinki, and most of them are targeted at families. The National Museum of Finland is a great example of that. The exhibition of the museum is dedicated to culture and lifestyle of indigenous people. Children will find many interesting and pleasant surprises there. They will be able to grind corn into flour, build a wooden house or learn how to type on an ancient typing machine.

Suomenlinna Fortress is another interesting cultural object, which ancient walls hide a lot of interesting. There are several awesome museums in the fortress, and in summer visitors can see performances of an open-air theater. Besides that, travelers will find workshops of a potter and a glass man. A walk in Suomenlinna will be interesting for children of school age.

LeikkiLuola Playground located on Hakaniemi Square is a true paradise for little fidgets. This entertainment center works all year round. Inside, children will find colorful trampolines and labyrinths, a rock-climbing wall and playing rooms where kids can play with Lego construction kits. There is a special room for kids below 3. Travelers with children will be pleased to visit the Murulandia Theme Park, where children will enjoy special learning games, charming playhouses and labyrinths. Older children will be more interested in visiting the interactive museum. Meantime, adults are welcome to relax in a special area with a comfortable café.

Cuisine & restaurants

Cuisine of Helsinki for gourmets. Places for dinner best restaurants

The national cuisine is a kind of "fusion" of Eastern and Western traditions. Local culinary masterpieces will never leave any gourmet indifferent. Various vegetable stews and casseroles are considered popular dishes of home-cooking. When it comes to desserts, the locals prefer baking. Seafood is also very popular here, and many recipes of fish dishes strike with their originality and simplicity.

Salmon is one of the most popular dishes, which is offered to guests in any restaurant dedicated to Finnish cuisine. The dish is usually served with aromatic sauces and fresh vegetables. You can also find some Lappish dishes in the list of meals representing the national cuisine. Here venison remains a confident leader. This is one of major specialties, which can be tried only in elite restaurants. Finnish bread, which is baked for centuries according to a special recipe, deserves a special praise. Seeds, bran and sweet raisins are essential ingredients that are often added to it. Pulla vanilla muffins are the favorite dessert of local residents and tourists. Fruit and berry desserts also do not lose their popularity. Finnish chefs prepare wonderful puddings and shakes made of northern berries, so refusing to try these dishes is simply impossible.

In addition to restaurants specializing in national cuisine, there are really many diverse culinary destinations in the city. Chez Dominique restaurant was opened in 1998. It specializes in French cuisine. Among specialties of this restaurant are beef steaks and small pancakes with caviar. Resisting the aroma of the meals served here is simply impossible. Apart from national cuisine delicacies, Lappi restaurant is the best place to enjoy home cooking. It serves amazingly delicious cheese, roasted meat of northern deer, and fried whitefish is considered the specialty of the restaurant. Pannonia is the only restaurant in the city dedicated to Hungarian cuisine. Here guests can enjoy homemade pickles, meatballs with cabbage and lots of other interesting dishes, the best addition to which will be wine from the Pannonia's own cellar. Copyright

Helsinki is home to a unique café, Ekberg, which is recognized not only as the oldest café in the city but also in Scandinavia in general. This historic café has its own confectionery that has been operating since 1852. Needless to say, locals love to have their breakfast at this gorgeous café. In the morning, it often offers so-called "buffet type" breakfasts that include various meat delicacies and gourmet cheese, vegetable dishes, and nutritious pies. The confectionery makes excellent cakes and pies. Moreover, it bakes fabulous, mouthwatering muffins. There is a shop in the same building with the café, so visitors are welcome to purchase different types of chocolate candies, coffee and tea in beautiful gift packages, jams, and even mulled wine.

Fazer is a historic café that is also very popular with local people. This famous café has won love and dedication thanks to its delicious signature cakes. Every day, more than a dozen of different cakes are made at Fazer. It is also the right place to try traditional variants of cheesecake, signature berry cakes, mouthwatering chocolate cakes, and cute cupcakes. In the morning, this café also offers generous buffet type breakfasts.

In order to try more unusual and sophisticated dishes, consider visiting Juuri. The basis of the menu of this café is represented by Finnish cuisine. It is important to mention that chefs at Juuri offer a modern take on the classical national cuisine. Visitors usually order magnificent mushroom soup and rabbit cooked in accordance with a signature recipe. The modern café will certainly appeal to travelers who follow a healthy lifestyle and choose only healthy food. There is a separated menu for vegetarians and even guests who practice raw foodism.

Lohikeitto remains one of the most popular first course dishes in the national cuisine. The soup consists of salmon, cream, and potatoes. Local national cuisine restaurants also offer various types of kalakukko fish pies. Fine cuisine restaurants offer various dishes with trout, and graavi lohi is one of them. Quite an interesting fact fish is a popular ingredient of various salads. For example, rosoli is a delicious salad that contains herring.

Roasted venison is a typical local dish that, however, looks very exotic and unusual to tourists. The venison is usually served with cranberry sauce. Sara is another authentic Finnish dish that contains lamb meat. It has a very unusual cooking method. The meat is stewed for a long time in a special wooden pan. Thanks to that, the meat doesn't lose its original taste. Finally, it would be a mistake not to mention Lapland cheese with cloudberry that is available for sale in many grocery shops and large supermarkets in Helsinki.

Traditions & lifestyle

Colors of Helsinki - traditions, festivals, mentality and lifestyle

The locals are very hospitable, but they are distinguished by a certain restraint in communication. Great nature is considered the main wealth of their country. In the minds of local people relaxing holiday is invariably associated with a comfortable country house situated on the shore of a lake or a river. Sauna remains a favorite pastime for indigenous people. Here they can not only sit back and relax, but also communicate with their friends.

Owners of large apartments make a small sauna directly in their apartments. Each apartment building will certainly have a public sauna, which can be visited by all residents of the building for free. Local women are rather independent and willful. They are interested in politics and appreciate their independence. During a trip to a club or a disco you can see that sometimes women here behave as men. They can attend various entertainments on their own and be the first one who chooses a partner for dancing. Many bars and restaurants organize special ladies' nights several times a week. Men cannot attend such special events.

At first glance, the local people may seem quite serious and reserved, but they stick to official tone of communication only when they contact with strangers. In a company of friends, they are very cheerful and sociable. Independence Day, which takes place on December 6, is the most striking national holiday. Many interesting traditions and activities are connected with this day. Thus, in the morning a military parade takes place in Helsinki, and on evenings a grand ball is conducted in Presidential Palace. The national flag remains the main symbol of the Independence Day. On this day not only state agencies are decorated with flags; local residents hang the flags over the entrances of their houses. In the evening the square in front of the cathedral becomes the location of rallies. The celebration is finished with a large student march. Thousands of young people pass through central streets of the city. They light up torches that symbolize the beginning of a new free time. Copyright

In mid-June, the capital of Finland invites the guests from all over the world to celebrate its birthday together. Usually, the restrained and modest Finns organize a real annual festive marathon to honor the main city of the country. The center of Helsinki is filled with a cheerful flow of people, bright colors, and music. During the Helsinki Day, you will have major possibilities to enjoy various events for free! Moreover, throughout the years, this strictly local celebration became an international holiday. The celebration starts with a solemn ceremony on the Senate Square, which is held by the Mayor of Helsinki. One of the most popular events held during the Helsinki Day is the "Lunch in the open air". On the Pohjosesplanadi street, in the historical center of the city, stand a huge served table, behind which 1000 people are having the dinner. The cultural institutions of Helsinki play an important role in the festival. On June 12, all the museums of the capital open their doors for a free visit, when special excursions are held. Most of the events taking place on City Day in Helsinki are absolutely free.

Every year at the end of June, in the capital of Finland takes place the large-scale event LGBT Pride. This massive event is designed to support not only a tolerant attitude towards the LGBT community but also human rights and the civil equality of all people, regardless of their sexual orientation and gender identity. The participants of the festival gather in the

Senate Square of the city, preparing for the procession. Simultaneously with the Pride on Kansalistori Square, the International Euro Games take place. During these games, there are competitions for lesbians and gays in various sports. However, if you desire to take part in such sports competitions you are free to do that! Competitions are included in the program of the parade along with picnics, master classes, discussions, lectures, and discos that take place in different parts of the capital. In August, the kings and queens of the stage and geniuses of modern art cheer the public with the creative and positive energy. The annual Festival of Music, Visual Arts and Urban Art "Flow" is recognized and accepted by critics as one of the loudest events of the summer season in Helsinki. This festival of art combines many formats. As part of the Flow Festival, techno-rave peacefully gets along with an exhibition of paintings, a premiere of a documentary with a culinary tasting, and a jazz concert with performances or designer shows. A one-day ticket to the Flow Festival costs 70 euros.

In the last two weeks of summer, the city of Helsinki becomes the point for Finland's largest art marathon. The Helsinki Festival possesses very simple but important goals - to make art, in the broadest sense of the word, accessible to the masses. To achieve this mission, the organizers include the widest range of genres in the program of the forum: music (from classics and ethnics to heavy rock), circus, dance, fine art, sculpture, cinema, theater and much more. Annually about 300,000 residents of the Finnish capital and guests of Suomi visit the event under the aegis of the festival. About 20 of the best art institutions and concert halls of the city, including the Finnish National Opera, the Museum of Contemporary Art "Kiasma", the House of Music of Helsinki and the Design Museum, serve as the venues for the Helsinki Festival. The main concert stage - the tent of Huvila - is usually located in the parking space at the city water-front of Tokoyranta. At various times, such world stars as Radiohead, Massive Attack, Yoko Ono, Patti Smith and Laurie Anderson performed here. Each season within the framework of Helsinki fest passes about 500 large and small creative actions. The most significant event of the multi-festival holiday is the "Night of the Arts" (Taiteiden yö) - enchanting art carnival, with the participation of the largest museums, bookstores, theaters and cultural centers of the capital of Finland.

Culture: sights to visit

Culture of Helsinki. Places to visit old town, temples, theaters, museums and palaces

Senate Square remains one of the main points of interest in the city. The square is surrounded by beautiful buildings, the majority of which were built in the first half of the 19th century. There are also some historical monuments on the square, and in its center you can see a monument to the Russian Tsar Alexander II. The building of State Council, which was completed in 1822, is the most striking architectural place of interest in Helsinki.

Uspenski Cathedral is another prominent religious attraction. The age of the cathedral is around 150 years. The building is made of red brick, and the halls of the church are decorated with exquisite icons and elegant gilded iconostasis. Rock Church is, without a doubt, no less attractive. The church is located in Töölö district. Built in 1969, the church is one of the most original monuments of modern architecture. Carved in the rock, the hall of the church is distinguished by special acoustics. A dome made of copper and glass is considered the chief ornament of the church.

Sederholm house is a sight that is definitely worth making a visit. The house, which was built in 1757, is located in the historic district of Helsinki. Currently, the oldest building of Helsinki has become the location of a museum, which exposition is devoted to the history of merchant life. Among the cultural institutions of Helsinki we should definitely underline Arena Military Museum. Among its collections you will see valuable and historical documents, ancient weapons, uniforms, as well as many other interesting exhibits. Young visitors can attend special lectures, during which they can participate in military battles and learn many new facts about the medieval Finnish troops. Copyright

Outdoor rest enthusiasts will be interested in visiting Esplanade Park, the territory of which contains numerous interesting attractions. This is the location of a famous statue of a nymph. For many years the statue has remained the main symbol of the national festival of youth "Vapaa". The sea beauty is the symbol of joy and celebration. The opening of the monument took place in 1908.

To feel real awe while in the White City of the North (as Helsinki is often called), you can visit the Helsingin ortodoksinen hautausmaa cemetery. Here, both majestic monuments and beautiful buildings, including the amazing beauty of the chapel building, will immerse you in an unforgettable atmosphere that gives extraordinary tranquility. The cemetery was built in the beginning of the XIX century. Among the famous people who were buried here, it is worth mentioning Agafon Faberge and Yuri Repin. Another place that will be great for hiking is Länsisatama, where, it seems as though you can watch the sailing and floating ships for eternity.

The busiest place in the hometown of Tove Jansson is Hakaniemi Market; here you can enjoy the color, inherent only in the capital of Finland. And here is the subway station bearing the same name (that is, Hakaniemi) gained fame due to the shooting of a video clip rather than a film. The fact is that it was here that a sort of must-see clip of Freestyler performed by Bomfunk MC's was filmed. Another market Vanha Kauppahalli attracts tourists with its unsurpassed atmosphere. This does not seem like just any market building, but a gingerbread house. The attraction SkyWheel Helsinki attracts not so much by the fact that you can ride on it, but its extraordinary atmospheric uniqueness.

In the capital of Finland, there are a lot of interesting sculptural structures, among which it is worth visiting "Varsapuistikko" symbolizing maternal love, "Fazer Rooster" depicting the cock as a symbol of the famous confectionary brand, and "Haaksirikkoiset", which is a memorial in honor of those who died on the German military ship "Habsburg". Monuments to famous people have been installed too. For example, the sculpture "Topelius and Children", the monument to General Mannerheim, Jean Sibelius (located in the park named after him and ideal for a leisurely walk along a spacious area).

Quarter Torikorttelit is a great place for those who like to stroll through cozy streets with spacious cafes and restaurants, and look at Scandinavian-style buildings. A delightful architectural monument is Kampin kappeli. Besides the fact that this place is conducive for pacification, the architecture of the building is simply amazing. The place looks very unusual and as a result, attracts many tourists. There is a synagogue in the

White City of the North, which is also considered interesting from an architectural point of view. An excellent example of neo-Gothic architecture is Saksalainen kirkko. It is one of the most majestic buildings in the city, therefore definitely worth a visit by every tourist.

Attractions & nightlife

City break in Helsinki. Active leisure ideas for Helsinki attractions, recreation and nightlife

You will find the widest number of entertainment venues in Helsinki. Park Linnanmaki is the best place for family rest. In this park you will find more than three dozens of thrilling rides. In addition to this, the park is simply full of cozy restaurants and cafes, various stores and souvenir shops, as well as a large house-aquarium. The aquarium is home to numerous Baltic Sea inhabitants, as well as rare species of fish and shellfish imported from all over the world.

A visit to Heureka entertainment complex will be no less interesting. All of its expositions and rides are very curious and will be definitely loved by young travelers. During the tour you can learn a lot about the features of the human body, amazing natural phenomena and examples that show natural laws of physics. On the territory of the entertainment complex you will also find a park, where you will find rich exhibition of minerals. Tourists, who enjoy walking in beautiful places, are recommended to visit Esplanade Park, the main decorations of which are beautiful fountains and statues. Here are located several interesting restaurants. In the warm time of the year the park often becomes the venue for numerous music concerts and performances.

There are many nightclubs and discos in the city. Here absolutely every traveller will find a place to rest that will fit his/her taste perfectly. Kaarle XII is the oldest nightclub of the city. It was opened in 1976. The club will attract fans of various musical styles. Gourmet visitors will also like it, because next to the club is opened a great restaurant with the same title. Club

Helsinki is located in the shopping district of the city. Technical equipment of the club deserves the highest praise. In addition to enchanting music performances, here are often held fashion shows, presentations, and other interesting activities that will make the holiday even more diverse. Fans of "metal" music will be surely delighted by visiting the club named Hevimesta. Several times a week here are organized theme parties, and the club becomes the venue for concerts of well-known musical groups. Copyright

The best and most easy way to get acquainted with the capital of Finland and enjoy its attractions, as well as spring and summer atmosphere is by bike. We all know how European people are eco-friendly, and Helsinki is not an exception. In Helsinki, there is about 750 km of excellent bike trails, which can be reached almost anywhere. Worthy of attention is the bicycle route, for example, opened in 2012 Baana track length 1.3 km, which is laid on a former railway tunnel and extends from the Kiasma Museum seaside district Ruoholahti.

On the road, there are separate lanes for cyclists and pedestrians. Nearly 180 trees, 4000 shrubs, and perennial plants are planted here. The route is framed by massive rocks and stone walls built 100 years ago. On the road, there are places for recreation and works of natural art.

Near the hospital Maria, there are playgrounds for basketball, table tennis, and petanque. Under suitable weather conditions, Helsinki offers around 180 kilometers of trails. The best skiers cross the Central Park; they are supported, depending on the situation with snow, until late spring. At the hostel Paloheinä, located in the center of Helsinki, you can rent ski equipment and snowshoes. Near Helsinki, there are good slopes for lovers of alpine skiing and snowboarding. In all the centers, if necessary, you can rent equipment, as well as receive training at a ski school.

Rowing in Helsinki - is cool! To stay in the city, which is almost surrounded by the sea, without trying to swim on the canoe, or on a kayak - savagery! Here you will find many companies, which will gladly help you to get acquainted with the sea circle of Helsinki. Tourists and fans of fishing can also purchase a license for tourist fishing. The license includes fishing on tackle and spinning. There is the special territory equipped for fishing - Vanhankaupunki area, which is surrounded by water rapids. Licenses can be purchased at the Meri-Info booth, located behind the building of the Museum of Technology. Visitors aged 18 to 64 must also pay a state fee for fishing. If you are in Finland - you have no right not to try truly Finnish sauna. There are about 3 million saunas here. And all of them periodically melted regardless of the time of year. Finns soar at 100 ° C, which means that from time to time it's worth taking breaks to cool down. The easiest way is to dive into the lake or the sea, and in the winter - to plunge into the hole. As an option, puff up in the snow. If you intend to visit a real Finnish sauna, then leave a towel and clothes in the locker room and go to the steam room naked. In public saunas, as a rule, there are separate hours of work or own sections for men and women.

Other Attrations

Veuve Cliquot VIP Experience SkyWheel Helsinki

+358 404 804 604 / skywheelhelsinki@gmail.com
Located next to Helsinki's famous market square, the 40m high SkyWheel Helsinki offers magnificent views over the city and out to the islands in the archipelago, in climate-controlled cabins that ensure customers can enjoy the scenery throughout the year. In addition to their regular cabins, SkyWheel Helsinki also offers the more luxurious Veuve Cliquot VIP Experience, an extended 30 minute spin in their unique VIP-gondola, with leather seats and a glass floor. Guests are served a chilled bottle of Veuve Clicquot champagne to be enjoyed as the wheel slowly turns.

The Veuve Cliquot VIP Experience is a stylish option for special celebrations or corporate events. Guests are met at the SkyWheel Champagne Bar where they are welcomed to the SkyWheel, escorted to the VIP gondola, and served their bottle of Veuve Clicquot Brut. Inside guests sit in comfortable leather seats while relaxing music plays, the glass floor adding one extra view to enjoy. The luxury cabin is air-conditioned, so no matter the temperature outside guests are comfy inside. Perfect for groups of four, the VIP Experience costs 195€.

During the summer SkyWheel Helsinki has a relaxed summer terrace at ground level, while the champagne bar is open throughout the year, offering a wide range of refreshments. During the winter guests can warm up with a cup of coffee or hot chocolate while buying their tickets.

SkyWheel Helsinki opened in the summer of 2014 in Katajanokka, next to the famous the Market Square. The 40-meter-high SkyWheel offers magnificent views of the Helsinki archipelago and the city, while the 30 climate-controlled cabins ensure that visitors can enjoy the scenery all year round.

During the summer SkyWheel has a relaxed summer terrace at ground level, while the champagne bar is open throughout the year, offering a wide range of refreshments. During the winter you can warm up with a cup of coffee or hot chocolate in our shop while buying the ticket.

SkyWheel offers two special experiences:

- Veuve Clicquot VIP Experience offers an extended 30 minute tour in a unique VIP-gondola with four leather benches and a glass floor. Customers are served a bottle of Veuve Clicquot champagne to be enjoyed in the cabin. The price of the VIP Experience is 195€ for 1-4 people.

- Original SkySauna is SkyWheel's is newest adventure, which combines a unique sauna gondola with an amazing archipelago view and a comfortable hot tub on the ground. This amazing experience is not available anywhere else in the world!

Prices:
12€ / adult
9€ / children 3-11.v
Children under 3 years free of charge
Students and seniors 10€

Original SkySauna

Opened in July 2016, the Original SkySauna is a new and unique sauna experience, which combines a unique sauna cabin that reaches 40 metres, as well as a comfortable hot tub on the ground! In the sauna gondola you can enjoy the beautiful scenery of Helsinki and the archipelago, while in the hot tub you can admire the ships sailing by and the beautiful sea side.

The Original SkySauna has two separate dressing rooms, with en-suite toilets and showers, and a common lounge area and terrace for relaxing. Towels are included in the price, while bathrobes and sandals have to be booked separately. The SkySauna experience is specially designed for smaller groups, with a maximum of 15 people. The sauna gondola can accommodate up to a maximum of 5 people, while the outdoor jacuzzi can accommodate up to 10 people, while the rest of the group can relax on the terrace or in the lounge.

The Original SkySauna is great for a variety of events and special occasions, such as bachelor parties, birthday parties, company events, or even for groups of friends having a night out.

Prices are from 240€ for 1-4 person per hour. Additional hours are half price and additional persons 30€ per person.

10 Great Summer Activities for Helsinki

With a growing reputation as one of cultural hot spots of Northern Europe, Helsinki is a modern city that elegantly combines capital chic with outdoorsy adventures. Helsinki's urban heart is packed with great restaurants, lively bars, vibrant nightclubs and live music venues, while also being a city of museums and galleries, with public art in every neighborhood. Safe and excellently served by a well-connected public transport system, packed with open green spaces, Helsinki is also a child-friendly city perfect for family vacations. And at all times Helsinki is a city surrounded by forests, lakes, and the sea, with countless ways to enjoy adventures in the wild, making it a haven for outdoor enthusiasts. Here is a selection of activities and attractions that illustrate the variety available.

Helsinki SkyWheel and Original SkySauna

Having only opened in 2014, SkyWheel Helsinki has already become an unmistakeable feature of the harbour skyline, overlooking the market square and the open sea. The 40m high SkyWheel offers magnificent views over the Helsinki archipelago and the city, with 30 climate-controlled cabins to ensure visitors comfort all year round, with two extra special packages on offer. With the Veuve Clicquot VIP Experience visitors have an extended 30 minute tour in a unique VIP-gondola with leather benches, a glass floor, and of course a bottle of Veuve Clicquot champagne! The Original SkySauna Experience is a new and unique way to enjoy a sauna experience, combining a sauna cabin with a comfortable hot tub on the ground! During the summer SkyWheel has a relaxed summer terrace at ground level, while the champagne bar is open throughout the year, offering a wide range of refreshments.

The Mighty Suomenlinna Sea Fortress

Founded in 1748 and built by Augustin Ehrensvärd, Suomenlinna is one the largest sea fortresses in the world, and was made a UNESCO World Heritage Site in 1991. Occupying 8 separate, but connected islands, Suomenlinna is more than just a museum, it houses and maintains a thriving community of around 800 residents. There is much to see here, with exhibitions in Suomenlinna Museum, Ehrensvärd Museum, and in the tourist centre. The islands themselves are ideal for long nature walks, with six cafés and five restaurants, one with its own brewery, to sate all appetites. As popular with locals as it is with visitors, this incredible attraction is just a 20 minute ferry ride directly from Helsinki Market Square, with at least two ferries per hour throughout the day. Suomenlinna also hosts its own Jazz Festival and Blues Festival.

Didrichsen Art Museum

Idyllically tucked away on Kuusisaari island between Helsinki and Espoo explorers will discover one of Helsinki's finest private art museums. Originally designed as a summer villa with museum attached, Didrichsen Art Museum was built in two phases in 1958 and 1964, and today is home to a fine collection of works by artists such as Picasso, Miró, Kandinsky, Léger, Moore, Edelfelt, Schjerfbeck, and Särestöniemi. The museum also holds the only Pre-Colubian art collection in Finland, as well as a collection of Oriental art. The modernist buildings are surrounded by a delightful sculpture park set in well designed gardens, and are open to the public all year round. In the summer you can arrive at the museum via a ferry through the archipelago!

The summer exhibition 2018 at the Didrichsen Art Museum presents the work and history of the classic Swedish interior design company Svenskt Tenn. The exhibition runs from May 25th through to the 9th of September.

Living History in the Seurasaari Open-Air Museum

Another unique attraction worthy of a day out is the delightful Seurasaari Open Air Museum, the largest of its kind in Finland, located on a island in Helsinki. Showcasing all of Finland's folk history, Seurasaari recreates its traditional way of life through cottages, manors, farmsteads and churches, representing four centuries of rural life. Walking forest paths visitors can experience how Finns once lived, through their work, traditions, and celebrations; giving them a chance to experience everyday life from days long gone by. Walking around this peaceful rustic island, it is easy to feel as if you have stepped out of a time machine into a piece of living history. Informative, educational, and above all fun, Seurasaari is a real gem for Helsinki tourists, and absolutely perfect for a family day out.

StopOver Finland's Sibelius Experience

Culture vultures can get a taste of Finland's most celebrated classical composer, Jean Sibelius, in the Kalsallissali or National Hall, a national romantic gem situated in the heart of Helsinki on Alekanterinkatu. This authentic cultural experience is available daily in one of the city's most distinctive buildings, and lasts one hour. Talented musicians perform some of Sibelius' most impressive compositions Finlandia, Kuusi, Romance, Rondino, and Valse Triste on grand piano and violin. The concert is enhanced by a visual show where nature images and graphic illustrations by Erik Bruun, are projected onto screens. Following the concert, guests receive a Sibelius Finland Experience gift CD, a special booklet, as well as a celebratory nonalcoholic beverage to drink with the musicians.

Room with a View the Clarion Hotel and SkyBar

One of Helsinki's newest and most modern hotels, the 16-floors-high Clarion Hotel Helsinki, located by the sea in Jätkäsaari, isn't just one of the best places to stay, it is also one of the very best places to relax and take in a view. At the top of one of Helsinki's tallest buildings guests and visitors will discover the luxurious and classy Sky Room, commanding spectacular views over the city. Tastefully decorated in Nordic chic, with artwork by both young Finnish and international artists, the Sky Room is one of the coolest meeting points in Helsinki. Make yourself comfortable, relax and take in the view, while enjoying drinks created by experienced bartenders, or perhaps something from their range of fun and surprising snacks! Clarion Hotel Helsinki is also home to the Kitchen & Table concept restaurant by Marcus Samuelsson, that combines traditional Finnish ingredients and local traditions with Manhattan flavours fun dining that focuses on social eating, an open kitchen and an urban atmosphere.

Getting Back to Nature in Nuuksio National Park

Some visitors to Helsinki might be pleasantly surprised to discover one of Finland's finest national parks is just 30 minutes away! Covering some 53 km2, Nuuksio National Park provides an easily accessible escape from urban life into the wild where typical Finnish scenery can be enjoyed. There are a number of specialist service providers operating in and next to the national park, offering a wide range of experiences. These include guided excursions, sauna experiences, hiking, foraging, fishing, and canoeing. Visitors wishing to stay longer can choose from hotel rooms and apartments, lakeside cabins and villas, camping, and even suspended tents! Visitors to the park should definitely check in the newly constructed Haltia Nature Centre, where they can learn more about all 40 National Parks.

Lake Tuusula's Art Walk

Just 15 minutes from the airport and 30 from Helsinki city centre, a trip to Lake Tuusula provides visitors with an opportunity to experience Finland in miniature. When taking a stroll along the lakeside through this beautifully tranquil landscape, it is difficult to believe you are so close to the capital. Lake Tuusula's natural beauty attracted many Finnish masters of art, music, and literature to the area; visitors taking the Tuusula Art Walk get to experience the golden age of Finnish art, brought to life in the many house museums along the way. Lake Tuusula provides excellent opportunities for all kinds of activities, the outstanding natural scenery is best explored by either cycling or hiking the route that circles the lake. Of course, the lake itself is ideal for rowing and kayaking, sailing, fishing, and swimming.

Explore the Archipelago Sea with the HopOn Bus to Kimitoön

Another great idea for a day trip or longer is to catch the HopOn Bus from Helsinki to Kimitoön Island in the Archipelago Sea. The journey can be combined with any number of fantastic experiences, sights, local food, and accommodation. Highlights of the trip include Bengtskär, the tallest lighthouse in the Nordics, Rosala

Island's authentic Viking village and centre, historical pilot's islands, Örö Fortress Island tucked away in the Archipelago National Park, the quaint island village of Högsåra, and the fascinating interesting visitors' centres at Söderlångvik, Kasnäs, Sagalund, and Bjärkas.

Cruise the Baltic with Silja Line

Another great option for visitors to Helsinki is to further explore the Baltic capitals with a day trip to Tallinn, or a two night trip to and from Stockholm, on Silja Line cruise ship. These luxurious ships provide great activities, for kids and adults alike, as well as entertainment, and fantastic dining choices the Stockholm trip also has a spa and fantastic duty-free shopping opportunities. Tallinn is just two hours away, leaving you a whole day to explore the medieval city sights, before returning in the evening.

Tips for tourists

Preparing your trip to Helsinki: advices & hints things to do and to obey

1. Bargaining is not accepted in the majority of stores and shopping malls, but you can try to bring down the price a bit while walking in local markets.

2. It is not common to leave tips in hotels and restaurants of the city. As a rule, they are already included in the total bill. However, you can leave a reward of up to 1 EUR to doormen in restaurants and hotels.

3. The majority of hotels, regardless of their "star level", offers excellent service and well-equipped rooms. Tourists can easily choose not only hotels located in the city center, but also accommodations in more remote areas of Helsinki.

4. Travelers, who make vacation with their family, are provided with favorable discounts. This mainly concerns hotel accommodations, excursions and value-added services in hotels.

5. Smoking is prohibited in public places, so when you make a booking, it's better to negotiate this question in advance. Copyright

6. Local residents are very concerned about the environment. Therefore, any negligence can cause large fees.

7. Tourists are recommended to carry an identity card or a hotel card as it helps avoiding many troubles.

8. Various home decorations remain the best souvenirs from Helsinki. Each mall provides a great selection of handmade carpets, as well as handicrafts made of wood and ceramics. You can also consider buying leather goods. Here this material is used for making items of different styles and trendy showy accessories.

9. Shopping fans are best to visit the city during Christmas holidays. At this time of a year all malls offer enormous seasonal sales.

10. If you plan to make a trip to woods, make sure you wear tight clothes and have a treatment against insects. Then nothing will spoil your pleasant walk.

Unusual weekend

How to spend top weekend in Helsinki ideas on extraordinary attractions and sites

The large market that works every weekend on the central square of Helsinki is well-known beyond the borders of the city. However, the old roofed market of Wanha Kauppahalli is often neglected by travelers. The structure of the market is very unusual one can see beautiful wooden stands with fruit and vegetables, with compact cafes open opposite to them. These cafes are the reason why experienced travelers visit the market as they are among the few places where it's possible to try classic national delicacies fish, local cheese, best sorts of beer, and real homemade baking. If you visit this amazing place, don't forget to try sandwiches with shrimps and caviar, while sweet tooth travelers are recommended to purchase a jar of blueberry jam, maybe even more than one jar you will not be disappointed.

Continuing the gastronomic theme, it is important to mention some advantages of the abovementioned market square. This is where visitors can try the most delicious smelt and roasted salmon in the city while waiting for a ferry or searching for memorable souvenirs. Small open stalls work all year round on the market square. These stalls cook and sell the delicious local "fast food". The taste of the fish that has been just removed from fire is nothing but splendid. The fish is served with a choice of garnishes, such as French fried potatoes or vegetables.

If you want literally to diversify your acquaintance with the city and its culture, make a ride on an unusual train known as Kulttuuriratikka. That's an informal name of route 7A train. For many years the tram has been used for various culture events. Numerous music concerts and exhibitions take place directly in its carriages, so such a ride promises to be an interesting one. The unusual tram with a red sculpture on its roof is not hard to distinguish from regular trams. The culture tram can be seen on weekdays from 15:00 to 18:00. Don't be afraid about the price the ticket costs just as much as other trams do. Copyright

If after an exciting day full of entertainment you're not in a mood to return to your classic hotel, it's high time to make a ride to Kylmäpihlaja Lighthouse. Built in 1953 and located on a rocky island, the lighthouse is still in action. Travelers have a unique opportunity to sleep in a comfortable guest room that is open directly in the old lighthouse. It takes only 45 minutes to reach the distant island by ferry from Helsinki.

Many people who walk in the most famous park of Helsinki, Esplanadin, have no idea about an amazing place of interest that is right under their feet. Several years ago Helsingin Energia Company started building the new district cooling system underground. The system is expected to be finished in 2015, so very soon the large cave will be filled with water, but as of now visitors can go down and walk in winding tunnels. The atmosphere in the cave is quite mysterious and it is skillfully decorated with artistic lighting.

If the above-mentioned attractions are still not enough and you crave for something more thrilling, it's time to visit the most extreme place of the Finnish capital - Linnamiakki Park. This park will fit the bravest visitors as there are no colorful rides in this park only scary looking metal constructions. Without a doubt, Kingi freefall tower is the most thrilling ride in Linnanmaki, so everyone is welcome to experience how it feels to fall from a 75m height just don't forget to fasten the belts.

Climate

Helsinki has a humid continental climate, with significant moderation from the sea and it's the coldest major city in Scandinavia and one of the coldest cities in Europe. Winters are damp, snowy and cold and temperatures usually stay below freezing and temperatures can fall down to -7°C (18°F) in February (the coldest month). However, Helsinki is located in the extreme south of Finland meaning that below -20°C (-4°F) temperatures happen 3-4 times a year at most. The record low is -35°C (-31°F). Snow typically lies on the ground from late December to late March but the season can have significant variations from year to year and when temperatures rise slightly above freezing it can transform into a gray slush.

Spring and autumn aren't well-defined as cold weather can persist into May (the average low is 6.3°C or 43.3°F) and it can start as early as October.

Summer is when the people of Helsinki are most active. However it can feel much cooler to people from the rest of Europe (especially Southern Europe) as the average high is a mild 21°C (70°F) but the mercury can dip down to 14°C (57°F) during the night and occasionally down to 10°C (50°F). This doesn't mean though, that Helsinki isn't affected by warm air masses from the south leading to 25°C+ (75°F) temperatures during the afternoon but being moderated by the sea. The record high is 32°C (90°F).

Accommodation

Extraordinary hotels

Best choice for your unusual city break in Helsinki

Best Western Premier Hotel Katajanokka

From Helsinki center - 2.2 km
Without a doubt, Best Western Premier Hotel Katajanokka remains the most creative and easily recognized hotel in Helsinki. It is located on Katajanokka Island, where the hotel occupies a historical building of a former prison that dates back to 1837. Former cells for prisoners were turned into comfortable guest rooms, and some parts of the building have almost completely maintained their original atmosphere. One of the halls with massive brick walls and grating has become the location of Jailbird restaurant. When the weather permits, visitors of the restaurant can seat on the comfortable open-air

terrace. Among extra amenities offered by such an unusual "prison" hotel in Helsinki, travelers will find a sauna and a gym that works round the clock.

Radisson Blu Seaside Hotel, Helsinki
From Helsinki center - 1.6 km
Radisson Blu Seaside Hotel, Helsinki is also quite an unusual and attractive hotel. Radisson Blu Seaside Hotel has become famous mostly thanks to its original design. The décor of guest rooms and public spaces is made exclusively of natural and eco-friendly materials, and that's why Radisson Blu hotel in Helsinki possesses the honorable title of an eco-hotel. All rooms are made in different styles and are decorated with bright furniture and giant paintings of luxury cars, seaside landscapes, and local landmarks. The hotel has its own restaurant named Viola that, besides everything else, has a wonderful play zone.

Original Sokos Hotel Vaakuna Helsinki
From Helsinki center - 0.6 km
A very interesting and symbolic hotel, Original Sokos Hotel Vaakuna Helsinki was built in 1952 to provide

space for guests of the Olympic Games. Nowadays, the high-class hotel belongs to the list of Helsinki attractions and shares the building with the famous Sokos shopping mall. As all guests of the hotel get a special 10% discount in Sokos, Original Sokos Hotel Vaakuna Helsinki is very popular with fans of shopping.

Sofia House Helsinki
From Helsinki center - 6.5 km
The luxurious Sofia House Helsinki also occupies an honorable place among hotels in Helsinki. This high-class cottage can provide space for up to 8 people at once. The three-storey villa is located not far from Korkeasaari Zoo and is surrounded by a large well-groomed garden with comfortable terraces perfect for relaxation and a barbecue area. Sofia House Helsinki will be certainly liked by travelers who enjoy staying in the country area. The villa is well-equipped and comes with everything needed for a comfortable stay. There is a charming living room with a fireplace on the ground floor.

Hostel Erottajanpuisto

From Helsinki center - 1.3 km
Budget travelers can also stay in an unusual setting if they choose to book a room at Hostel Erottajanpuisto. This modern hostel is considered one of the most modern and stylish accommodations of its type in the city. The design of Hostel Erottajanpuisto is based on skillful dark wood décor. The natural splendor of the interior is underlined by bright carpets and colorful bed clothing, and thanks to large windows all rooms are very bright. It is worth noting that the hostel is open in a beautiful historical building that is located only several minutes away from picturesque Esplanade Park.

Eurohostel
From Helsinki center - 2.2 km
When describing unusual budget hotels in Helsinki, Eurohostel is worth a close attention. Guests of this hostel are welcome to stay in comfortable single or double rooms with modern design that only adds to quality relaxation and a peaceful aura of the place. In the morning, a delicious buffet style breakfast is served

for guests of the hotel, and in the evening everyone is welcome to relax in the cozy restaurant and try the best sorts of Finnish beer. The modern hostel has a quality sauna, bike rental, and many other services, the choice of which in Eurohostel is really great for a hotel of such category

Stylish Design Hotels

Stylish weekend in Helsinki collection of top unique boutique hotels

Hotel Klaus K

From Helsinki center - 1.1 km

It is safe to say that Hotel Klaus K is one of the most famous designer hotels in Helsinki. The hotel's concept and its inimitable décor are inspired by the Kalevala epic poetry. The interior is based on beige and golden shades and is supplemented by beautiful artistic lighting. Magnificent details made of light wood are a distinguishing feature of the hotel's design. Besides classic style rooms, there are several creative guest rooms at Hotel Klaus K, including car rally inspired rooms and special colorful rooms for romantic and passionate guests.

Cumulus Hakaniemi
From Helsinki center - 0.9 km
Cumulus Hakaniemi will also please its guests with an unusual style of its rooms that are mostly made in bold colors. Light hardwood floors, walls painted in deep blue shades, large windows, and modern soft furniture it won't be hard to enjoy a comfortable stay in such a setting. Many travelers prefer to stay in rooms located on the top floor they are distinguished by mansard ceilings and windows that only add to a cozy atmosphere of the hotel.

Hotel Finn
From Helsinki center - 0.9 km
Many affordable hotels are also distinguished by a pleasant and creative design, and Hotel Finn is one of them. Its rooms are made in different styles and color combinations, but all guest rooms feature comfortable crisp white beds and dark wood furniture with clean lines. Premium wallpapers in bold colors with

interesting patterns, lamps of different shapes and sizes, original paintings, chandeliers, and big mirrors these accessories help creating a truly inimitable setting. Among extra services offered at Finn, it's impossible not to mention a wonderful library with a wide choice of books in different languages of the world.

Next Hotel Rivoli Jardin
From Helsinki center - 1.3 km
The designer hotel Next Hotel Rivoli Jardin never ceases to prove its title of a paragon of style and elegance. The beauty of its rooms is hard to describe in words. White dominates in all guest rooms but that doesn't mean that all rooms look alike or boring. Crisp white walls, retro style furniture, white flowers in graceful lamps, and transparent curtains on large windows the rooms look very natural and authentic. Elegant pattern on the walls and colorful paintings only add to the refined style of this wonderful hotel. Next Hotel Rivoli Jardin also features some designer

elements, such as unusual lamps, vases, and stone sculptures.

Radisson Blu Royal Hotel, Helsinki
From Helsinki center - 0.9 km
Radisson Blu Royal Hotel, Helsinki is targeted at fans of modern luxury. Guest rooms at this hotel are made in different styles, so travelers are welcome to book a creative room with round shaped windows or a spacious suite with colorful furniture. The skillful use of textiles of different textures, from graceful semitransparent curtains to heavy fur blankets on the beds, remains one of the main secrets of the inimitable design. State-of-art lighting adds special charm to the public areas of Radisson Blu Royal Hotel.

Scandic Paasi
From Helsinki center - 0.8 km
Open in 2012, the designer hotel Scandic Paasi has quickly gained worldwide popularity thanks to its non-standard design. The hotel is made in accordance with the most authentic national traditions. Fans of boxing, music fans, and connoisseurs of the culture of the past

will easily find a suitable room at this hotel. Guest rooms feature creative wallpapers with thematic patterns, textiles with typical national motifs, and modern designer accessories. The ground floor of the building features a beautiful relaxation area with floor-to-ceiling windows. Guests can rest on colorful sofas and cute bright ottomans. Active travelers will be glad to know that Scandic Paasi has a free bike rental and provides equipment for Scandinavian walking.

Luxury and fashionable hotels

Top places to stay in Helsinki
Hilton Helsinki Kalastajatorppa
From Helsinki center - 3.9 km
The high-class Hilton Helsinki Kalastajatorppa is targeted at luxury travelers, who are guaranteed to have a quality relaxation in the atmosphere of absolute comfort and sumptuousness. Guests will enjoy spacious rooms with panoramic windows and king size beds, a quality private garden, and a wonderful adjusting territory. Gourmet visitors are recommended to have a lunch or dinner in Meritorppa restaurant,

where they can try delicious national dishes while admiring the panoramic view of the coast. The hotel's garden is also a place where visitors can relax in a serene setting, and active travelers might prefer to use the bike rental service.

Hotel Kämp
From Helsinki center - 1.1 km
The prestigious Hotel Kämp is open in one of the most beautiful historical buildings in Helsinki. Among the advantages of the hotel, it's simply impossible not to mention the high-class spa center with Turkish steam bath and sauna. Health lifestyle followers are always welcome in the modern 100 square meter large gym at Hotel Kämp. Every day, special yoga and pilates sessions are organized for visitors of the gym. When it comes to "gastronomic travel", Hotel Kämp is simply flawless here. The exotic Yume restaurant serves finest Asian cuisine, and the hotel's bar is a wonderful place to try the best sorts of local beer.

Citykoti Downtown Suites & Penthouse

Apartment hotel Citykoti Downtown Suites & Penthouse is also worth the closest attention even of most discerning guests. This hotel offers only 6 stylish apartments. Every apartment comes with a modern kitchen, a large TV, a DVD player, and even a small sauna where guests can relax at any convenient time. The hotel's roof has been partially turned into a wooden terrace. Citykoti Downtown has a convenient location as it takes only several minutes by foot to reach Kampi shopping mall and various restaurants.

Original Sokos Hotel Presidentti Helsinki
From Helsinki center - 0.6 km
The luxurious Original Sokos Hotel Presidentti Helsinki will never disappoint even hard-to-please guests. Its spacious guest rooms with lots of daylight are distinguished by elegant décor. The design of rooms and public spaces includes many wooden details. The hotel provides many extra services for its guests, including access to a large indoor swimming pool with natural daylight. When darkness falls to the city, head to Sevilla restaurant & bar, where guests are treated to

sangria, a traditional Spanish beverage, and magnificent tapas snacks. Adjutantti sports bar is the right place to watch thrilling sports competitions, while fans of shopping will be pleased with a 10% discount in the nearby Sokos mall.

Holiday Inn Helsinki City Centre
From Helsinki center - 0.5 km
The upscale Holiday Inn Helsinki City Centre is open close to the main railway station. This hotel is targeted at fans of different types of sport and offers a ton of services for travelers with children. The hotel's design is made in the traditional Scandinavian style, so expect to see skillful wooden décor and natural textiles. There is a high-quality playroom with kids' furniture that will be liked by travelers with children. Moreover, families will be pleased to known that children are provided with free breakfasts at Holiday Inn Helsinki City Centre.

Hilton Helsinki Strand
From Helsinki center - 1 km
Tourists, who want to enjoy elite services and spend their vacation in the atmosphere of absolute comfort,

will like Hilton Helsinki Strand. The large relaxation area on the top floor of the building is the most unusual element of the hotel's infrastructure. It includes a sauna, a gym, and an indoor swimming pool. Gourmet travelers are familiar with Bridges, an elite restaurant with opulent signature dishes made of salmon and venison. On Saturdays, the hotel traditionally hosts a magnificent buffet type dinner

Hotels with History

Preserved history of Helsinki: long-standing and historical hotels
Radisson Blu Plaza Hotel, Helsinki
From Helsinki center - 0.7 km
Radisson Blu Plaza Hotel, Helsinki is the most famous and popular historic hotel in Helsinki, which has been serving guests since 1917. The hotel is located just a couple of minutes away from the central railway station and magnificent Kaisaniemi Park. Guests of Radisson Blu Plaza Hotel, Helsinki can choose from more than 300 comfortable rooms, all of which are made in modern style and feature bright accessories

soft furniture, pillows, and textiles of turquoise, lilac, and pink shades. All guest rooms come with exclusive Magic Dream beds and a choice of pillows that can be selected by travelers. The hotel is famous for its Michelin awarded Kitzen restaurant that serves international cuisine and HUB bar that works round the clock.

Glo Hotel Art
From Helsinki center - 1.3 km
Glo Hotel Art is also distinguished by an inimitable historic atmosphere. This hotel is open in an eye-catching building in a modern style not far from the center of Helsinki. Glo Hotel Art offers stylish rooms with rich décor and modern electronic equipment. Some rooms come with state-of-art acoustic systems, while in others guests will be fond of a comfortable work area and a thoughtful lighting system. Among interesting peculiarities of the hotel, it is worth noting interesting décor of public spaces that still keep the original elegance. Artistic wooden ladders with banisters, interesting lamps and a spacious hall with a

fireplace everything reminds of the graceful culture of the beginning of the 20th century. The ancient wine cellar of the building has been turned into a magnificent restaurant where guests can try the most popular dishes from Scandinavian cuisine.

Solo Sokos Hotel Torni
From Helsinki center - 0.9 km
The historic Solo Sokos Hotel Torni is well-known to fans of art and music. This hotel draws the attention of its numerous guests not only because of a wide choice of colorful and comfortable rooms but also because of an interesting entertainment program. The charming pub of the historic hotel is a regular venue for various music concerts and thematic shows. Don't forget to get to the top floor of the building and have a drink in the stylish bar of Solo Sokos, Ateljee. A visit there will be interesting not only for fans of exotic cocktails but also for art lovers. For many years the bar has been chosen as a venue for exhibitions and presentations.

Seurahuone Helsinki
From Helsinki center - 0.7 km

Seurahuone Helsinki is open in an elegant building that dates back to 1913. The interior of the elegant hotel also reminds of the culture of the past. Stylish designer retro style furniture is perfectly combined with massive glass chandeliers, and giant paintings together with furniture made of premium sorts of wood create the atmosphere of aristocratic elegance. Don't forget to attend Socis bar the unusual venue is located under a glass cupola and is decorated with a fountain and La Havre beer restaurant.

Scandic Grand Marina
From Helsinki center - 2 km
The prestigious Scandic Grand Marina will also conquer hearts of guests with its inimitable historical atmosphere. This high-class hotel is open in a large-scale and unbelievably beautiful building in modern style and with centuries-old history. The hotel is open near a lively waterfront, not far from Uspensky Cathedral and the city center, so Scandic Grand Marina is considered one of the best places to stay for travelers with children. Many of its rooms are intended

for families with two-level rooms being especially popular with guests. It's important to mention that both guest rooms and public spaces are made of natural and environment-friendly materials. That is why Scandic Grand Marina enjoys the title of an eco-friendly hotel. Free access to sauna and gym would be a pleasant addition to your vacation in Helsinki, and children will fall in love with a special open-air playground.

Legends Hotels

Helsinki legends. Famous hotels glorified by history or celebrities

Glo Hotel Kluuvi
From Helsinki center - 1.1 km
Glo Hotel Kluuvi is particularly popular with guests of Helsinki. Only a several minute long walk separates the hotel from the central railway station and Galleria Esplanade shopping mall. The high-tech hotel with stylish interiors is well-known far beyond the borders of the city. All of its rooms feature a plasma TV, a hi-end audio system, and an air conditioning system. The

hotel has become particularly popular thanks to Kämp Spa that features different massage rooms and a relaxation area with comfortable lounge chairs and pleasant lighting.

Apartment Hotel Aallonkoti
From Helsinki center - 0.3 km
A large choice of apartment hotels is one of distinguishing features of Helsinki, and Apartment Hotel Aallonkoti occupies top ranks in that list. Stylish apartments with modern electronics and equipment are made in black-and-white and feature panoramic floor-to-ceiling windows. Each apartment comes with an iPod dock station, washing and drying machines, and a big plasma TV. Some apartments are intended for travelers with children, and so they have two-layer beds and various toys.

Omena Hotel Helsinki Lönnrotinkatu
From Helsinki center - 1.1 km
Omena Hotel Helsinki Lönnrotinkatu remains the leader among midscale hotels in Helsinki. It keeps attracting visitors with an optimal combination of

affordable prices and high-quality service. All guest rooms feature minimalist design and beautiful wooden décor. The electronic equipment of apartments makes the hotel suitable for a long-term stay. Omena Hotel Helsinki Lönnrotinkatu has won the devotion of thousands of travelers because of a large choice of rooms, so both single travelers and groups of tourists will find a suitable room there.

SATO HotelHome Lapinlahdenkatu
From Helsinki center - 1 km
The famous SATO HotelHome Lapinlahdenkatu is located in the picturesque district of Kamppi. The hotel offers more than 70 fully equipped apartments for its guests. SATO HotelHome differs from other apartment hotels by a wide range of services. For example, guests have a free access to a high-class fitness center and sauna. There is also a wonderful playground for children in the territory of the complex. Travelers with children will be pleased to some about some extra services at SATO HotelHome Lapinlahdenkatu, including installation of an extra bed.

Scandic Simonkenttä

From Helsinki center - 0.7 km

Scandic Simonkenttä is a stylish hotel that is open in a modern and good-looking building with panoramic windows. This hotel has won love and devotion of thousands of healthy lifestyle fans. Spacious rooms with wooden floor and furniture are just one of the advantages of this magnificent hotel. The eco-friendly hotel offers free rental of bikes and special equipment for trekking. Every morning, a delicious buffet type breakfast is served for guests of the hotel with all the dishes served being made of organic products. It is also worth noting that the diversified menu includes special dishes for diabetic guests and travelers on a diet.

Original Sokos Hotel Pasila Helsinki

From Helsinki center - 2.6 km

Located somewhat away from the lively city center, Original Sokos Hotel Pasila Helsinki is also one of the most popular hotels in the capital of Finland. Besides beautiful rooms made in red and white colors, the hotel offers a range of exciting services. There are squash rackets courts in the territory of the hotel, besides that guests get special discounts for visiting the nearby gym, EasyFit. Finally, gourmet travelers are recommended to pay attention to Sevilla restaurant that serves Spanish cuisine, and in Böle bar visitors can try the most famous sorts of local beer and wine.

Romantic Hotels
Helsinki for couples in love best hotels for intimate escape, wedding or honeymoon
Fabian Hotel Helsinki
From Helsinki center - 1.5 km
Travelers, who plan to have a romantic break away in Helsinki, are recommended to pay attention to Fabian Hotel Helsinki . The stylish and graceful atmosphere of the hotel is perfect for a peaceful vacation. All guest rooms are spacious and made mostly in pastel colors. Large king size beds, soft sofas and armchairs with premium upholstery, big panoramic windows and an adjustable lighting system create a truly inimitable atmosphere in the hotel. All guests of Fabian Hotel get complimentary welcome gifts fruit baskets and flowers.

Crowne Plaza Helsinki
From Helsinki center - 0.6 km
The premium Crowne Plaza Helsinki is open near the building of Finnish National Opera. This hotel has absolutely everything needed for a comfortable and interesting weekend or vacation. Crowne Plaza can be proud of its wellness center with a giant indoor swimming pool, and in the spa visitors are welcome to attend massage rooms or relax in the sauna. When it's dinner time, it's hard to find a better place than the romantic Macu restaurant where visitors can try best Merranean delicacies and premium wine. Travelers who prefer more unusual places are recommended to head to Fidel pub that is distinguished by an inimitable national atmosphere.

Best Western Hotel Rantapuisto
From Helsinki center - 10.1 km
Romantic couples who simply want to relax in a peaceful setting will hardly find a better place than Best Western Hotel Rantapuisto that is open in the picturesque neighborhood of Vuosaari not far from the

coastline and a beautiful forest. This hotel offers functional rooms made mostly in cream and coffee shades. Guest rooms also offer breathtaking views of the surrounding landscape. In order to make a stay in this romantic hotel more diversified and exciting, guests are recommended to visit Itäkeskus shopping mall, one of the biggest shopping malls in whole Europe, which is located nearby or make an unforgettable cruise. It is worth noting that the hotel has a private beach that is perfect for peaceful evening walks.

Essexhome Apartments
From Helsinki center - 2 km
Essexhome Apartments can be probably called the most romantic apartment hotel in Helsinki thanks to its design. Spacious guest rooms are decorated with large beds with carved headboards and crimson bed clothing, national style paintings, and flower bouquets. Rooms also feature such creative designer accessories as bright carpets and ottomans, pillows of different colors, and interesting lamps of various shapes and

sizes. Such a thoughtful design with attention to even slightest details and modern equipment of apartments provided by Essexhome allow enjoying a romantic and comfortable vacation.

Traveller's Home is a pleasant place with a charming atmosphere. The apart-hotel is located close to the famous Stockman shopping mall. Guests of Traveller's Home are provided with numerous services that can make any vacation more exciting. All clients of the hotel can visit City gym free of charge and attend the tanning salon with a 50% discount. Guest rooms are distinguished by a cozy home-like atmosphere. Moreover, there is a beautiful garden close to the hotel.

Apartment White Orchidea
From Helsinki center - 7.7 km
Apartment White Orchidea is the right choice for travelers who crave for a vacation in a luxurious and peaceful atmosphere. A mere view of the historical building of the hotel gets visitors into a romantic

mood. All rooms are made in black and white shades and all of them feature interesting paintings. The apartments also come with a fully furnished hotel with amazing views of the surroundings. Fans of open air activities are always welcome to attend the adjusting garden. Apartment White Orchidea is a good choice for tourists with children as there is a wonderful playground in the territory of the hotel.

Shopping in Helsinki

Shopping in Helsinki authentic goods, best outlets, malls and boutiques

In Helsinki, there are a lot of interesting places for shopping. Stockmann is the city's most famous shopping complex. This is the largest department store in Scandinavia, which opening took place in 1926. It occupies a very beautiful historical building. In fact, this huge department store takes a whole city block. It's difficult to imagine a category of goods that can not be purchased in it. In a spectacular historical building, there are more than one hundred clothing stores.

There are brand footwear shops, cosmetics and perfumery, numerous jewelry stores and shops offering household goods. In the most popular department store in Helsinki, you can buy excellent souvenirs and visit popular restaurants and cafes.

Market Square will be the best place for morning shopping. As well as several hundred years ago, nowadays, an excellent market runs here. The best time to visit it, is so close to the regular big holiday. During the warm season, fresh fruits and vegetables are sold here, as well as excellent farm products. On Christmas Eve you can buy popular sweets, traditional holiday souvenirs and jewelry. For many years, fescinating markets and entertainment events have been regularly held at the Market Square.

Those who want to turn shopping into a fascinating walk, should go to Esplanade boulevard. It originates near the Market Square and houses dozens of popular shops, restaurants and hotels. It is here, that the Arabia brand store is located, which offers exclusive products made of glass and porcelain. Stylish clothes can be found in Marimekko store. To purchase luxury bed linen and home textiles, go to Finlayson store. On the boulevard, there is a decent choice of souvenir shops. Frugal tourists will be pleased to learn that prices in most stores always remain at an attractive level. Copyright

Lovers of gastronomic shopping should go to the Old Market Square. Here, is an old covered market, which looks more like a museum. This beautiful historic building hides one of the most interesting and popular food markets in Helsinki, where the best national products are sold. The market offers a large choice of fruits and vegetables at any time of the year. They also sell fresh seafood, elite meat and venison. Farmers from around Helsinki offer the best home-made sausage, cheese and other popular home-made products.

Those who prefer stylish shopping centers, should go to the Forum center. It presents more than a hundred fashion stores of famous brands, including H&M and Jack&Jones, as well as Backstreet and Benetton stores popular with youth. In the shopping center you will find some large sporting goods shops. The Body Shop popular cosmetics store is also here. The complex is beautifully decorated. It has several cosy cafes, where you can relax after shopping.

Fans of walks through antiquarian markets will be interested in spending a day in the Hietalahti Square. Here, runs the largest and most interesting city's Flea Market, the variety of goods on which is simply amazing. Here, you can buy antique copper utensils, rare vintage books, jewelry, as well as a lot of other interesting antiquities. It is important to note that all the items on this market are of high quality. This place is loved by collectors and connoisseurs of antiques from around the world.

Lasanic Luxury Retail Store

Lasanic is a high-end retail store located in the centre of Helsinki on Fabianinkatu close to many of the city's famous landmarks.

Lasanic is a luxury retail store occupying 1500 square metres right in the heart of Helsinki, just around the corner from the capital's iconic Senate Square, and close to many of the cities most famous landmarks. Lasanic is located in an architecturally significant building, the interior of which was designed by the famous Finnish architect, Alvar Aalto.

Lasanic is renowned for delivering the highest possible service to its customers, as befits a retailer selling some of the biggest and best known high-end brands in Europe. These include Montblanc, Suunto, Pandora, Victorinox, Samsonite, Lipault, Skagen, Bering, Lamy, and many more. The unique jewelry, watches, and luxury accessories combined with their famous service helps Lasanic stand out as an excellent shopping experience. There is also a cozy Moomin Café on the premises, where visitors can relax with a coffee or snack and feel themselves transported to the idyllic Moominvalley loved by some many around the worl

The End

www.ingramcontent.com/pod-product-compliance
Lightning Source LLC
Chambersburg PA
CBHW031102080526
44587CB00011B/781